The Falklands Play

THE FALKLANDS PLAY

a television play

IAN CURTEIS

HUTCHINSON
London Melbourne Auckland Johannesburg

First published in Great Britain in 1987 by Hutchinson Ltd,
an imprint of Century Hutchinson Ltd,
Brookmount House, 62–65 Chandos Place, London WC2N 4NW

Century Hutchinson Australia Pty Ltd
PO Box 496, 16–22 Church Street, Hawthorn, Victoria 3122, Australia

Century Hutchinson New Zealand Limited
PO Box 40-086, Glenfield, Auckland 10, New Zealand

Century Hutchinson South Africa (Pty) Ltd
PO Box 337, Bergvlei, 2012 South Africa

British Library Cataloguing in Publication Data
Curteis, Ian
The Falklands play.
I. Title
822'.914 PR6053.U76

ISBN 0-09-170611-4

Set in Linotron Sabon by
Rowland Phototypesetting Ltd
Bury St Edmunds, Suffolk

Printed and bound in Great Britain by Richard Clay Ltd,
Bungay, Suffolk

DEDICATED
TO THOSE BRITISH SERVICEMEN
WHO GAVE THEIR LIVES
IN THE FALKLANDS CAMPAIGN

ACKNOWLEDGEMENTS

A considerable number of people have been generous with their time and knowledge over this play.

In particular, I would like to thank the Attorney General, Sir Michael Havers; Admiral of the Fleet Lord Lewin, CDS in 1982; Sir Anthony Williams and Mr John Heath, our Ambassadors to Argentina and to Chile in that year; Mr Nicholas Ridley MP, Mr Cecil Parkinson MP, and others.

Admiral D. R. Sherval and his staff at Fleet Headquarters, Northwood; Admiral Guy Liardet, Commander Trevor Dale, Mr G. R. Palmer, Mr John Ledlie, Mr Robert Moore and others at the Ministry of Defence. Mr Graham Hands at the Foreign Office; and my good friend Captain Michael Parry, late Captain HMS *Antrim*.

Mr Anthony Whittome, of Century Hutchinson Ltd, has been a fountain of patience and sound advice since first approaching me in May 1985, seeking to publish the play coincidentally with its BBC-1 transmission. I owe a great debt to Mr Cedric Messina and Mr David Giles, respectively producer and director of the play (until cancellation) for a wealth of professional expertise and advice.

Most of all, I should like to thank my wife Joanna Trollope for her unstinting support and loving patience, even when at one point, asleep, I apparently called her Mrs Galtieri.

IAN CURTEIS

Ian Curteis (b. 1935) read English at London University and started his career in the theatre as actor and director, working around most of the repertory theatres in Great Britain. He was invited to join the BBC as a staff director in drama in 1963, and directed Z-CARS, KIPLING, THE WEDNESDAY PLAY (including plays by John Betjeman, John Hopkins, William Trevor) before moving to ITV to direct FRONT PAGE STORY and childrens' adventure series. He also directed a feature film THE PROJECTED MAN.

In 1966 he turned to full-time writing, which has included the following television plays: BEETHOVEN (BBC-2), SIR ALEXANDER FLEMING (BBC-2 and the BBC's entry at the 1973 Prague Festival), MR ROLLS AND MR ROYCE (BBC-2), LONG VOYAGE OUT OF WAR (a trilogy of full-length plays on BBC-2 later published by Calders), THE FOLLY (ATV), THE HAUNTING (ATV), SECOND TIME ROUND (ATV), H. E. BATES ADAPTATIONS (Granada), A DISTINCT CHILL (BBC), THE PORTLAND MILLIONS (Granada), PHILBY BURGESS AND MACLEAN (Granada; ITV's entry at the 1978 Monte Carlo Festival, BAFTA nomination Best Play of the Year, subsequently transmitted in 48 countries with viewing figures totalling over 100 million.)

Also such series as THE REGIMENT, DOOMWATCH, OWEN M.D., Z-CARS, BARLOW AT LARGE, SUTHERLAND'S LAW, CROWN COURT, SPYTRAP, JUSTICE, THE ONEDIN LINE, HADLEIGH, THE CEDAR TREE, THE DUCHESS OF DUKE STREET, etc., Originator of ROUGH JUSTICE (BBC 1979) and, with Joan Curteis, of THE PRINCE REGENT (BBC 1979). PEOPLE LIKE US (six episodes adaptation R. F. Delderfield novel, LWT 1978). THE RUDOLPH HESS BUSINESS (STV play for ITV, shot on the original locations, ITV entry 1979 Commonwealth TV Festival), THE ATOM SPIES (ITV).

CHURCHILL AND THE GENERALS (BBC-1; Grand Prize, Best Programme of 1981, New York International Film and TV Festival; BAFTA nomination Best Play of the Year), SUEZ 1956 (BBC-1; BAFTA nomination Best Play of the Year), MISS MORISON'S GHOSTS (ITV; ITV entry 1982 Monte Carlo Festival; nomination USA Emmy, New York 1982).

1981/2; screenplay of MAN'S FATE (Malraux's La condition humaine) to be directed by Irvin Kershner as a major feature film; and a trilogy of plays for BBC-1 about Bernard Berenson and Lord Duveen: BB AND JOE.

Play: A PERSONAL AFFAIR, starring Virginia McKenna and Gerald Harper, Globe Theatre Shaftesbury Avenue, opened June 1982.

Treatment for a screenplay for Sir Richard Attenborough of TOM PAINE, the intended companion-piece of GANDHI. Screenplay of Graham Greene's THE MAN WITHIN (for Channel Four). Adaptation J. B. Priestley's LOST EMPIRES (Granada) in eight hours.

STALIN, treatment for a screenplay for YTV (ITV), THE TRIALS OF LADY SACKVILLE (2 × 75′ plays for BBC-1), THE FALKLANDS PLAY, a three-hour play for BBC-1.

EUREKA – the opening six hours of the first Euroserial, coproduced between Germany (ZDF), Italy (RAI), UK (C.4), Austria (ORF), Switzerland and France, to be shown simultaneously in all six countries.

Currently: an eight-hour adaptation of William Shirer's THE NIGHTMARE YEARS (Germany 1934–41) for HBO, New York.

Ian Curteis lives in Gloucestershire with his wife, the novelist Joanna Trollope, two sons and two step-daughters.

INTRODUCTION

On October 22 1982, the newly appointed Director General of the BBC, Mr Alasdair Milne, addressed a session of the now-defunct Writers' Luncheon Club. The venue, I remember with some pleasure, was the Members Room in the London Zoo, which has a good view of the crocodiles.

He made a vigorous speech about television drama, in the course of which he spoke generously of my play *Suez 1956* – a three-hour play which occupied most of one evening of BBC-1, with an interval for the Nine O'Clock News. The leading role had been Sir Anthony Eden; the Cabinet, Nasser, Eisenhower and Dulles had all been major parts, all played by actors.

At home that night, I wrote him a brief note of thanks for what he had said, tucked it into a signed copy of the play (it had by then been published) and sealed the package.

A few moments later I came back, unsealed it and added a postscript: 'In a few years' time, I would like to write a similar sort of play about the Falklands Crisis' – re-sealed it, took the dog out for a moonlit, bedtime walk, and posted the parcel.

Not long afterwards, an enthusiastic reply came from Alasdair Milne. He was commissioning the play *now*, he said, and was putting the necessary wheels in motion without delay.

I was alarmed. The fighting had only been over a few months. I am not in the business of throwing together instant drama, just pour on water and stir. Some form of dramatized documentary was just about possible, perhaps, but a *play* . . . ! – with historical perspective, characterization, jokes, showing human vulnerability, people losing their tempers, emotion – with all the originals of my characters still alive and sitting there watching on the night – no, it was surely far too soon. It would be impertinent.

In the same moment, the showman in me also spoke up. What a challenge! – a play about the incumbent Prime Minister and her Cabinet – passionate, partisan, dealing with some of the issues and principles I care about most strongly. And, after all, the Director General himself had commissioned it.

Would Shakespeare, I thought, lying awake that night, have written *Hamlet* differently, had he been able to lunch with Polonius? (Athenaeum or Garrick?) Would Ophelia have demanded casting approval?

I consulted my old friend Sir Harry Boyne, former Chairman of the Parliamentary Lobby, much respected and held in great affection by both sides in Westminster. His advice was exactly what I had started to realize myself: now you've given them the idea and they've got the bit between their teeth, if you won't do it, they'll get someone else.

So, taking a deep breath, I asked my agent to open negotiation on the BBC's opening contractual gambit.

Negotiation took six months. Not over money – the advance of royalties was agreed at the outset – but over other matters. I would not undertake such a highly sensitive play without cast-iron safeguards; after all, it would be my copyright, I would be morally and legally responsible for what it said, and if the axe fell it would be on my neck. I am not a hired scriptwriter.

I obtained a strict right of consultation from the BBC which gave me an effective right of veto on all major casting and on choice of director (two ways in which a play can be heavily biased without altering a single word of dialogue). The BBC guaranteed to transmit the play as a single piece – which was essential, to give the emotional build-up to the leading character; it could not be episodic, or this mounting emotional steam-pressure would be punctured and dissipated.

Above all, the BBC agreed to a clause undertaking that they would make it absolutely clear in all publicity and on-screen announcements that the work was a play and not a dramatised-documentary. I have for some years insisted on that as a *sine qua non*; if the company won't agree, then I don't write the play. Confusion between those two distinct categories has caused untold anger and distress. It need not be.

I asked Keith Williams, the Head of Plays, if Cedric Messina, one of the most distinguished of BBC Plays producers, for ten years producer of the BBC's prestigious Play of the Month, would produce it. He readily agreed. Messina and I discussed at length the style in which I would construct the play, and in which it would be produced.

We agreed at the outset that, in casting, we would not be aiming at 'look-alikes', a walking Madame Tussauds. We would cast eminent actors and actresses of approximately the right age, type, forcefulness of character (or otherwise), with perhaps one or two identifying features, who would then play 'straight'. In other words, *impersonation* would not be attempted.

By this stage, the deal had been done. The contract was signed on April 6 1983.

After some months finishing a play for ITV, I began work. There was already a vast amount in print, and I started to read up and try to marshal this mass of material; but for a play one needs above all to get to the human side of things. The historical playwright is not trying to put over the facts in an objective, drama-documentary sort of way, but to get into the characters' heads and hearts and emotions, to show them as real, all-round, vulnerable human beings, acting sometimes instinctively, sometimes illogically, responding to the strange, volatile inner music of real human relations.

For this it was essential to meet and get to know some of the people most centrally involved in the Falklands conflict.

One of the most extraordinary but marvellous things about this country, is how easy it is to get to see people. Anthony Sampson says in the introduction to his *Anatomy of Britain* that he wrote to the 200 most powerful people in the country, asking to see them and discuss what they were up to. 197 complied without hesitation. That is also my experience – but in this case, I was to run full tilt into a thunderstorm.

I sought and obtained, sometimes through friends, sometimes by direct application, access to various people in the Ministry of Defence and the Cabinet Office. Almost immediately, I was hit by a Force Nine Gale. Tempers still ran hot and furious over the BBC's alleged behaviour during the conflict itself, less than a year before – the BBC (I was heatedly told) was directly responsible for the deaths of British servicemen, they broadcast propaganda for the enemy, they put the cruel fascists of Argentina on the same footing as the British . . . a disgrace, Goebbels-like, arrogant, disloyal . . .

It was the selfsame storm that Alasdair Milne had himself encountered during the crisis, when he and the then BBC Chairman George Howard had been howled and shouted at by over one hundred furious MPs in Committee Room 13 at the House of Commons for what was regarded as traitorous behaviour. 'They were kicked all round the room,' said one MP. 'Theirs was the most appalling, lamentable, disgraceful performance. There was no apology or contrition.'

No play can be written in the teeth of such gales of hatred. I rang Keith Williams, and later lunched with him at Consolidated Productions (who were seeking to co-produce a trilogy of mine with the BBC). He agreed with my suggestion that time should be allowed for tempers to cool, and matters fall more into perspective. For all I know, he may also have felt that it was too soon anyway.

So I got on with other commissioned plays, taking me to New York, Moscow and over much of Europe. I adapted J. B. Priestley's *Lost Empires* for Granada; Graham Greene's *The Man Within* for Channel Four; a treatment of *Tom Paine* for Sir Richard Attenborough, the proposed companion-piece to *Gandhi*; the same for *Stalin* for ITV; two plays on *The Trials of Lady Sackville* for the BBC, and other projects in development.

It is not always realized that a television playwright like myself has, at any one time, about a dozen projects at some stage of development. He has to, to cope with the chaotic system. Some have been written and are going into production; others may be at the initial stage of reading-up and sketching out ideas to see if there is a play there at all. Some may lie fallow for a couple of years, and then abruptly leap to life as the production company changes its schedules yet again (often for reasons outside its control – a fluctuation in its advertising revenue, a lurch in sterling/dollar exchange rate, affecting much-needed American co-production finance) and it is suddenly pitchforked into production, entailing hastily arranged weekend meetings with producer and director, and attendance at previously unscheduled rehearsals or filming, cutting right across what you were supposed to be writing for someone else, across family holidays and sensible working schedules worked out after church on quiet Sunday mornings.

Time passed. I remained in touch with the producer, Cedric Messina, who stayed a tower of strength throughout, as I knew he would. More books poured out about the Falklands crisis. The Ponting trial came and sensationally went. Lord Franks reported. Tam Dalyell's accusations were minutely examined by an all-party Foreign Affairs committee of the House of Commons, and found wanting. The turbulent air began to calm.

By the beginning of 1985, I felt the time was probably growing towards ripeness. I cleared the decks, as far as possible, and began work for a second time.

Nothing had prepared me for the sheer galvanizing absorption of the subject. I couldn't wait to get to my desk each morning. Just as the crisis itself touched a central nerve in the nation's psyche in 1982, so it electrified me. This was not shallow jingoism, but the dramatic rising to the surface once more of values and issues that we on these islands have cared most profoundly about down the centuries, and on which our civilized freedom rests.

I saw as many of the key figures and places as I could. The Attorney General, Sir Michael Havers, Admiral of the Fleet Lord Lewin, Chief of Defence Staff in 1982; Sir Anthony Williams and Mr John Heath, our Ambassadors to Argentina and Chile at the time; Mr Nicholas Ridley MP, Mr Cecil Parkinson MP, Admiral David Sherval and many others, all were generous in the time they gave to answering my questions, in person, on the telephone and by letter.

All the *facts* I took strictly from authoritative printed sources; but theirs were the illuminating anecdote, the human touch, the sudden telling flash of character that John Aubrey would eagerly have scribbled down.

I was also allowed to see some of the key places: parts of Ten Downing Street I had not previously visited, the Foreign Secretary's room in the Foreign Office, Chequers itself one fine sunny afternoon, the Prime Minister's quiet, still room in the House of Commons, the secret underground War Room of Fleet Headquarters in North London, from which the war was actually fought – all the locations crucial to the play. Much of this took a long time while I was – very properly – checked out, and references taken up. Television playwrights are not easy for the security services to categorize.

There was, by now, a simply colossal amount of raw material to master – Hansard, the Franks report, the entire *Times* coverage of the crisis, five or six biographies, analytical articles and profiles of my leading characters by the ton, several weighty and authoritative tomes, countless paperbacks. I read every word in print, took sackfuls of notes and Xerox copies; and sought to discover amidst this blizzard of raw fact that shape that would tell the story, allow the *people* to emerge within a dramatic (in the technical sense) framework, and would grip and inform and excite an audience of, perhaps, 15 to 20 million people, for one whole evening, just as I had been excited.

I am one of those lucky people who knew what he wanted to do when he was fourteen. Life becomes much simpler then; you know where you have to go. As part of the essential training, as I saw it, I went into the theatre after university, and spent many years as a working actor. The Master Plan said this should be two years; Master Plans never work out, and many were the twists and turns before I shouted Enough and turned to full-time writing on my thirtieth birthday.

It is a curious thing, but when one has spent night after night, year in year out, acting before a live audience, an instinct is born that is never lost: I cannot now write a line without knowing exactly what effect it will have on the audience – not just laughter and tears, but all the infinite, silent fluctuations that an audience goes through, sitting out there in the darkness, as if the umbilical cord between us still existed.

Those in television drama whose feet and foundations are in the real, live theatre, never lose this; those who came up on the electronic or administrative side of television have little sense of it. Drama, to them, is an intellectual, calculated thing; an audience, something one reads about in the ratings.

My craft is a very ancient one – certainly 2,500 years old, probably more. It is essentially the craft of *construction* – of the play itself, of individual scenes, of characterization, of single lines, of humour strategically placed. I spend over half my time on any play working on its construction, going endlessly over lines and scenes, trimming, tightening, highlighting, juggling, always seeking to produce the illusion of economic effortlessness, always remembering how an actor will do it and what he will bring to it – all in longhand, here at my desk in my silent room in our house in Gloucestershire. The only sounds are when I try lines and scenes out loud, this way and that, and, rarely, the quiet tip-tap of the typewriter as I finally pull a sequence together that seems at last to be 'running sweet', as they say round here of full ditches.

And out of this hard, lonely but fascinating labour, nine till six-thirty on weekdays and half-a-day most weekends, slowly emerges (one hopes) over many months and several drafts, a play, a living, breathing thing with its own heartbeat.

In April 1986, I delivered the fourth draft to the Director-General and the Producer. It was warmly received. Plays (Organizers) unit was instructed to slot it into production with all speed, for recording in January and transmission on BBC-1 on April 2 1987 – the fifth anniversary of the Argentine invasion. It would be a three-hour play, 7.30–11 p.m., with a thirty-minute interval for the Nine O'Clock News. It was to be a major event.

I was in touch with Organizers unit, or it with me, almost daily over the next few weeks, to ensure I was going to be in the country and available for the production (I was at that stage commuting to Munich). Other productions were re-scheduled and switched about by Programme Planning Department to make way for *The Falklands Play*, first at BBC-Bristol, then in London.

Full rehearsal and studio facilities finally crystallized and were firmly booked (studio TC-1, the BBC's largest studio, January 24 to February 8 inclusive), even down to re-set-and-lighting days; detailed budgeting was completed by the Programme Associate and approved; Cedric Messina was officially assigned, and signed his contract which specified *The Falklands Play* and his own production dates September 29 1986 to April 30 1987. (All these details are important, because of the BBC's later insistence that 'there had been no commitment to the production of this play'.)

On June 2 I went to see Alasdair Milne to put him in the picture about whom I had seen and the opposition I had initially met (which I had already outlined to him in a letter). We met in his panelled office, in Broadcasting House, at 4.30 p.m.

He was his usual cheerful, vigorous self. Three weeks previously, he had written to me, 'I am reading the play at the moment.' It therefore seemed a fair question to ask if an election would affect production, and I did this almost immediately.

He thought about it for a moment, nursing his white wine; then said it didn't seem to him that it would matter. 'She will hold out as long as she can – probably till 1988. The earliest an election *could* happen, barring some national catastrophe, is autumn 1987. I don't see that transmission in April presents any problem.'

We talked of other plays I wanted to write – one about the Munich crisis, for the fiftieth anniversary in 1988, another about Cecil Rhodes. He was enthusiastic in his response; but nothing came of them.

There was a telling moment. At one point he crossed away to refill his glass. I asked if this had been John Reith's office. 'Yes,' he replied, 'there was a fireplace there.' He tapped a panel with his foot. 'A man used to bring up the coals.' 'Does Reith haunt the place?' I asked. There was a pause; his back was to me as he replenished his drink. He eventually replied, tersely, with what seemed to me a wry sadness, 'He used to.' Ichabod, ichabod.

The BBC Contracts and Copyright Department had meanwhile written to me, officially accepting the text of the play in the full legal and contractual sense, subject only to any comments the producer Cedric Messina might later have.

We worked on the fourth draft together. I had been a bit carried away by the fun of 'Haigspeak' – the strange, convoluted English that General Haig sometimes employs. The role of General Galtieri could be improved, he pointed out, by some passing reference to his background, and a line or two more about his frequent drunkenness. With Cedric's expert help and tactful guidance, I pulled these and many other points into final shape.

As the director, he proposed David Giles. I was delighted. He is best known to the public for *The Forsyte Saga*, *The Mayor of Casterbridge*, and *The Barchester Chronicles*, but his distinguished career spans thirty years. He read the script, said he would love to do it, and could make himself free for the now fully booked production dates.

Cedric proposed him to the new Head of Plays, who gave his official blessing and approval. We were assembling an exceptionally strong team.

Thus enter stage right a pivotal character in this story, the new Head of Plays, Peter Goodchild. I regret having to introduce a personal note at this point, but to do so is essential if subsequent events are to be understood.

I have worked with seven Heads of Plays, over twenty-three years. The previous six have all been distinguished play producers, directors or, in one case, a playwright. All have spent a lifetime in drama, on television and in the theatre. Peter Goodchild is the first since the post was instituted to have none of these advantages.

He is a graduate in Chemistry, and has spent most of his career in the Science Features Department of the BBC. While head of that department, it produced some dramatized-documentaries on essentially scientific subjects, a form of adult education. I hope the reader will by now have accepted (if he was not already fully aware of it) that such things are a million light-years from a play.

Not long after his appointment, it became clear that Plays Department was in turmoil. The main factor responsible was Peter Goodchild's institution of a new system of countersigning virtually all producers' decisions before they were valid. By this method, he would frequently refuse to sanction, or overrule, the judgement of some of the most experienced drama producers in British television.

Whatever the aim of this new system, it caused a massive escalation of resentment and a plummeting of morale. By the way it was executed – frequently without explanation – it appeared to many that their new, inexperienced Head of Plays regarded his own dramatic, artistic or administrative judgement as superior to their own. Had it produced outstandingly better results, much might have been forgiven. But I've seen or heard of nothing to suggest it had, in the press, from friends, or from my own observation.

A parallel might be if someone who had spent all his life in the theatre and television drama was suddenly appointed Head of Science Features Department, and insisted by his actions that his *scientific* judgement was superior to all the PhDs and prize-winning documentary makers with long and excellent track records that composed that department.

Peter Goodchild and I had clashed several times, particularly over a commissioned trilogy of plays of mine on which I had spent a year of my life. It was called *BB and Joe*, and was set in London, Paris, New York and Florence in the 1920s. Producer, director and myself were the team that had originated

Churchill and the Generals. Here, we felt, were three linked plays that would be intelligent, prestigious and popular entertainment – the BBC's answer to *The Jewel in the Crown*. Generous American co-production finance was available. The co-producers had written to Peter Goodchild no less than five times, they told me, expressing their eagerness to go ahead. But when he suddenly cancelled the entire project, he did not feel any necessity to explain why to any of us. Our reactions, both personal and professional, can be imagined. For seven months we requested some explanation. Finally, he gave us two reasons, of such breathtaking inadequacy that we couldn't at first believe he was serious.

These, then, were the already choppy waters, when *The Falklands Play* sailed over the horizon.

I immediately decided that it was essential to build bridges and proffer olive branches; not because I felt inclined to do so – quite the opposite – but because it was essential that the *BB and Joe* experience was not repeated. Trouble must be anticipated and nipped in the bud. So I invited Peter Goodchild and his wife to lunch with me and my wife at our house in Gloucestershire, hoping that by sheer hard work in a social atmosphere, we might be able to forge some *modus vivendi*.

Soon after the lunch had been fixed for June 20, Peter Goodchild rang me up twice. He expressed pleasure at the invitation, and then started raising points in the script.

This took me aback. It is a very strictly observed and universally accepted professional practice never, under any circumstances, to attempt to bypass producer and director in such a way, and quite wrong for an administrator with no *locus standi* to try to tamper with the text. But I was in the business of building bridges, so I listened.

I could not for some time see the point of what he was saying. He always speaks very quietly, and plays his cards close to his chest. Behind a façade of courtesy, the cool calculations of ambition are not difficult to perceive. He appeared to be sounding me out about how strongly I felt over certain aspects of the Prime Minister's character, particularly her private and vulnerable self in contrast to her more public Iron Lady self. Over certain speeches which touch on this, and on the Falklands conflict being other than a manifestation of mere shallow jingoism, he said more than once, 'We'll see about that' – as if he was in the role of an Editor, which he is not. When I asked him *why* he was raising such points and tried to pin him on evidence (the play is meticulously researched) he immediately backed down.

He floated one other matter. In the second conversation, he said, quite casually, 'By the way, I'm thinking of replacing Cedric as Producer.' I said nothing, but the moment we hung up, rang Ruth Messina (her husband had just left for some filming in Kenya) – established that he knew nothing of this – then made two quick calls: the first to his agent to warn him what was afoot; the second to the previous Head of Plays, Keith Williams, who expressed deep concern at any attempt to lever Cedric off his own production, and replace him, presumably, with someone more biddable.

What then happened behind the scenes, I cannot say; but this attempt to remove one of the most experienced and fairminded producers the BBC has, after three years on the play, did not succeed.

These two conversations with Peter Goodchild were the first occasion I had that uncanny feeling I was to experience several times over the next few weeks: the shadowy presence of someone else, staying hidden for the moment, for whom Goodchild was acting as messenger-boy. For if these were his own ideas, why did he not produce evidence, or argue a case for them?

But who could this be? Not Michael Grade, I thought, then Controller of BBC-1. He had been in the USA during production planning, but had returned, and at a key meeting in his office on the 6th floor of Television Centre, at 10.15 a.m. on Friday 6 June (four days after my meeting with Alasdair Milne) had given his official go-ahead for the production. Cedric Messina had rung me jubilantly after the meeting; the Plays Department (Organizer) Trevor Noakes had confirmed more detail later in the day, as did two others present. That was the official send-off; no reservations there.

That left me with the other front runner, Bill Cotton, Managing Director BBC Television. A man of passionate loves and hates of people, in both public and private life, he often calls himself 'a backroom boy', modestly playing down his position as ringmaster of Television Centre. Son of the late Wakey-Wakey bandleader and showman to his fingertips as he is, I had often admired the monumental restraint he must have to clamp over his passions in order to fulfil the provisions of the BBC Charter relating to balance and impartiality. I remembered the torrent of feeling about Anthony Eden he had poured forth to me over my play *Suez 1956*, when we viewed it together in 1978, not one drop of which he had subsequently shown in public.

Having an instinctive dislike of dealing with people who hide behind others (if this was indeed the case) I put through two calls to Bill Cotton's office, on June 12 and 16, to say I would appreciate a brief word with him about *The Falklands Play*. He was not able to speak to me, and the calls were not returned. I later wrote, but he never replied.

On June 18, Peter Goodchild's secretary rang to say that he and his wife would no longer be coming down to lunch with us on the 20th, 'as Peter says it no longer seems worth his while' – a curious phrase, not noticeably helpful to social detente. A few days later she rang again, to ask if they could come down on July 7 instead, but unable to explain this remarkable U-turn. I agreed to the 7th; what I said to my wife in private is best not recorded.

On July 2, Goodchild rang up once more. He was, he said, just about to go in to see Bill Cotton about *The Falklands Play*. Would I tell him *exactly* what had transpired at my meeting with Alasdair Milne? Slightly surprised (would Cotton not have known?) I told him in full. Goodchild pressed for details, which I gave him.

At one point he said, 'Oh, there are the people before me coming out, I must be quick' – the first indication I had that he was not in his own office – but showed no signs of hurrying the rest of our conversation. The reader will see the point of this, later.

Monday July 7 was a brilliantly warm and sunny day. We are lucky to live on the millstream of the River Coln, in one of the most gloriously unspoiled, heavily wooded valleys in England. Goodchild drove up the drive to our house at 11.30 – in a straw hat, smiling, and without his wife.

The press have made much of what might have happened that day, and a good deal of obfuscation about it has subsequently swilled about. In fact, it was perfectly simple. We drank some coffee, sat and talked in my offices, went for a walk, had lunch, walked and talked again, and he drove off about teatime. Apart from when my wife joined us for lunch, we were alone. We were both, I am sure, making a monumental effort to build bridges and bandage old wounds; the atmosphere was generally cordial; and if, at some points, surprising things were said, no one ever lost his temper.

The main thing I wanted him to see and understand was how a playwright like me actually *works*. The feeling in Plays Department was that he had no idea, that perhaps he thought a play was knocked together quite casually on a typewriter in one corner of the drawing room. Three rooms in my house are entirely given over to the process, which, given the sort of play I write, are in continual operation. I took him through to the archives and filing room, lined floor to ceiling on all sides with steel shelving and filing cabinets, bearing all the drafts and research and correspondence of all my 86 transmitted plays and series over 20 years, all the scripts and production files of the many plays I had previously directed when a television director with BBC and ATV, and of the 50 or so plays I had directed or acted in, in six years in the theatre before that, laying the foundations.

I showed him the successive drafts of *The Falklands Play*, how each evolved from the previous one, how this was actually *done*, all the little scraps of paper on which sentences were tried out and scribbled over and despaired about and shouted out loud and finally got right, the indexing process I'd invented so I can put my finger on the source for every single fact in each play. I showed him how I had built the Prime Minister's character from two detailed biographies and a fat file of serious newspaper interviews with her, lifting actual lines she says to get the right verbal rhythm (six foolscap pages of them), notes from her rare television interviews, and on the crucial fact that had dawned on me slowly but with increasing conviction: that the private, instinctive Margaret Thatcher is just as important *politically* as the public, logical one, but is far more rarely glimpsed.

He fingered over all this material as I explained it, with a gentle smile. I do not know what he was thinking, but his questions were curious: how many times did I go to see so-and-so, did we lunch together, who paid, how many times did we subsequently talk over the telephone?

After lunch, sitting down by the millstream with coffee, he started to raise points of script once more, as he had on the telephone. I immediately reminded him of the friendly stipulation in my letter to him of five days before (July 2): 'I'm sure you'll agree that [when we meet] it would be improper to discuss the *text* of the play without producer and director being present.' But he persisted, so I took careful note, without comment, of what he said.

These were his points:

(a) He felt 'unhappy' at those parts of the script that referred to what I have called the Prime Minister's private and instinctive self; for instance, her writing in her own hand to the relations of all servicemen killed during the fighting; her weeping quietly on the loss of the *Sheffield*; her showing private grief of any sort. He had no objection to the bellicose Iron Lady of the public scenes.

(b) He felt equally 'unhappy' at those speeches in the script that described the Falklands conflict as being fought to resist aggression, and thereby in a long tradition of such resistance that we, as a nation, have manifested again and again since the sixteenth century.

(c) He 'suggested' that I might consider rewriting some War Cabinet scenes to show Ministers taking into account what he called 'the coming election' when making military and political decisions during the crisis, and tailoring those decisions to the object of winning that election. It was, he said, naïve of me not to imagine that such things must have happened.

(d) He 'suggested' that I might write in a good deal more opposition to the Government's policies of sending the Task Force and fighting a hot war than I already had – in Parliament, in the press and country.

(e) He suggested that more explanation of Galtieri's frequent drunkenness might usefully be added. [This presented no problem, and was one of the points I had early agreed with the producer.]

I asked him for evidence. Point (c) in particular seemed to me dynamite. The sessions of the War Cabinet are particularly well documented. He was, it seemed to me, asking me to go substantially against the historical record *under my own name*, not his.

He could neither give evidence nor offer argument to support these suggestions. Anyhow, he added, they were just ideas for me to think about, ponder over.

Again I had the uncanny feeling that someone else was present, that he was not speaking for himself at all. Why else put such major suggestions forward, in the absence of producer or director, with no scrap of evidence or argument to support them? And what about the meeting with Bill Cotton on July 2, when he had rung me?

'What does Bill Cotton think about all this?' I asked. He immediately shifted, re-crossed his legs and threw me a nervous smile. 'We never had the meeting,' he said. 'When I got there, it was such a lovely day, he'd gone off to Wimbledon.' Then he added, 'I spoke to him briefly on his car telephone.'

It seemed to me the strangest statement. There was no subtlety in its execution – so much so, that in that split second I wondered if he was trying to signal something to me that he couldn't say openly. The radio-telephone detail seemed to be a quick afterthought.

On that note, he drove off. My wife and I had a large, stiff, early drink. We had achieved a somewhat strained cordiality with him; whether there had been any real progress on a professional level was another matter.

The following day, I wrote to him, briefly listing the script suggestions he'd made, and saying I'd look into them with producer and director. I knew very well what Cedric's reaction would be: without evidence, out of the question. He would go and see Goodchild and tell him that officially, and that way, the fragile detente I was working at, might be preserved.

What I didn't know as I wrote was that Goodchild had already raised these points with the producer, on July 4. He had rejected them as improper, political, unjustified, unbalancing the thrust of the play, and something he would have nothing to do with. Goodchild had been going behind his back.

Two days later, the bombshell burst. Goodchild had written to me on the same day, and our letters had crossed in the post. Safely back in Television Centre, he had written that his 'suggestions' were in fact mandatory – they *had* to be complied with, or the production would not proceed. His thanks to my wife for her hospitality and lunch were confined to a brief, curt, dictated, typed, six-word footnote.

It was the only time in this whole affair I lost my temper. I felt our hospitality had been abused, and that it was a cowardly act to write what he had not dared to say to my face. I replied thus (July 12):

'You introduce a new and disturbing element over *The Falklands Play*, which we certainly did not touch on when we met.

'You asked me to consider certain political additions to the text of the play . . .'

I then listed the main changes.

'As you know, every single fact in the present text can be verified from printed sources, and I would be wrong to add such important and new elements without good evidence.

'However, in your letter you say that these points "should be addressed *before we can go ahead with production*". This is an ambiguous phrase: the production is well on the road – producer contracted, director assigned and approved by you and me, budget completed, studio and transmission dates fixed for some weeks past.

'I would therefore be grateful for your categorical assurance that you do *not* mean "Unless you comply with these political points, irrespective of evidence, the production will be cancelled".

When this letter was published in the *Daily Telegraph* on October 17, I added this gloss:

'I am not an employed scriptwriter. I am a playwright, who owns the copyright in his own work and is responsible legally and morally for what it says.

'My contract of licence to the BBC specifies that they will make no changes to the text other than minor ones for the purposes of production. Mr Goodchild's proposals would radically have altered the nature and motives of key decisions of the War Cabinet, and would still have been transmitted as my work and my opinion.'

Peter Goodchild acknowledged but did not reply to this letter. Twice, in writing, I asked for his evidence. None was forthcoming. I made it clear that I would not make these politically loaded changes without evidence.

To make absolutely sure of my grounds over the main proposed change – the motives of the War Cabinet – I telephoned Admiral of the Fleet Lord Lewin, Chief of Defence Staff during the Falklands conflict, and wrote to Goodchild exactly what he said: (July 17):

'The suggestion you make was firmly rejected by one who was present at every single meeting of the War Cabinet during the crisis. No such consideration, he stated, ever played a part in the conduct of the war, when so many men's lives were at stake. At that stage, the election had not been mooted, and could have been up to two years four months ahead.

'He said he would be interested to know the source for your suggestion. I believe I have read everything in print on the Falklands crisis, and have never encountered the suggestion before. Perhaps you would kindly comply with my request to know on what you base it?'

He did not reply. Four days later, on July 21, the production was cancelled because of 'the next General Election' – the very reason the DG had assured me six weeks before would not affect production.

Two weeks later, on August 3, BBC-1 transmitted at peak viewing time a play entitled *The Queen's Arms*, by Alan Berrie. With respect to Mr Berrie, I do not think it is a very good play; but what was interesting about it was that it depicted the British during the Falklands crisis as drunken, nostalgic, flag-waving, bloodthirsty warmongers.

Four days before cancellation, it was obvious that matters were coming to a head. I made one final attempt to telephone Bill Cotton, and, this time, Michael Grade. Cotton never returned my call; Grade did, the following day.

I asked if he had any reservations about *The Falklands Play* – in fact to see if what he said chimed with Peter Goodchild's unhistorical 'suggestions', that I felt sure were coming from a third party.

It did not. He had four quite different points. Two of them were valid and I immediately agreed to them. The third was that he said I was not clear about the relationship between the sinking of the *Belgrano* and the timing of 'the Peruvian Peace initiative'.

It is, of course, a most important point. I replied, 'If I am not clear, then I certainly must be.' I later checked with producer and director, who assured me that the play was perfectly clear – the two events were unconnected. Grade had seemed unhappy about this. I was left wondering if he would have been happier had I showed them to be inter-dependent, in defiance of the very detailed examination and findings of the House of Commons All-Party Foreign Affairs committee enquiry into

Tam Dalyell's allegations, published on July 22 1985, which came to the contrary conclusion.

His other point was that he questioned the propriety of writing and producing such a play at all; to which I replied

(a) the Director General personally commissioned it, so he does not think so.

(b) British television is full of cruel caricatures of our elected leaders; what is so wrong with a play that treats them seriously?

(c) If the newspaper tattle of an election causes concern, why not proceed with the present production and recording, but postpone *transmission* until after such an election?

Cancellation followed before he could reply. On July 22, he wrote, 'In the light of the decision not to go forward, there is little point in extending our dialogue for the time being on this project.' The questions remained unanswered.

I was on the West coast of Ireland when the production was cancelled. Kind friends had lent us a remote, modern house two miles down an extremely rough stone track, on the rocks of Connemara overlooking the wild Atlantic. My wife and I, three of our children and two of their friends, adored it. There was no telephone. It rained. It felt like the Celtic rim of Europe, and all those early Irish saints made sense.

I lit the turf fire, and settled down to read my wife's latest novel, which, like all her books, rivetted me from page one, so that *Falklands Play* problems soon seemed pretty trivial.

The first sign of trouble came on a visit to the nearest post office, some five miles away. 'Ah Mr Curteis,' said the postmistress, pulling the plugs from the village telephone switchboard behind the single counter as we entered the little room, 'there have been three telegrams for you. After the first two, I realized it might be urgent, so I've given them to Mrs Behan who is coming past your place tomorrow for a funeral.' We tracked down Mrs Behan; the telegrams were small and green, as Irish telegrams should be. Their contents were such that we immediately drove three miles the other way to the nearest public telephone (still worked by crank handle), and, after some difficulty, got through to England.

My sister-in-law read me Alasdair Milne's letter, announcing cancellation. After more cranking and lengthy and persuasive conversations with operators across Ireland, I got through to Cedric Messina. 'How can they hope to get away with it?' he almost howled in anguish and disbelief, 'it's so obvious and brazen!'

After sleeping on it, Joanna and I went for a walk along the deserted white sands (we saw four people there in a week). I was going to fight it, I told her. I couldn't live with myself if I didn't. That play had to be got back into the schedules.

She supported me, as she always does, absolutely and totally. Her wisdom, diplomatic judgement and tact kept me on the rails more than any other factor in the extraordinary weeks that were to follow.

So we cut short our holiday, packed the two cars, and with the outraged and enthusiastic support of Tobit, Louise and Antonia (aged 20–14) drove back across green Ireland. Later, at a press conference, Michael Grade said I had been 'steaming mad'. This is untrue. All I felt was a profound and melancholy contempt, that a British institution as great as the BBC had once been, could act so corruptly. 'Does Reith haunt the place?' I had asked Milne. Pause, his back to me, replenishing his teatime drink. 'He used to.' Ichabod, ichabod.

Round one consisted of an exchange of letters between Alasdair Milne and myself. His first announced the cancellation. As editor-in-chief he has to take this decision personally in the case of major programmes, but his letter indicates those actually responsible.

The second letter lists the questions I believe I had every right to ask.

Broadcasting House, London. 21 July 1986
Dear Ian

I have had some discussion with Bill Cotton and Michael Grade about *The Falklands Play*. Both of them have reservations which will need to be discussed with you.

I wanted you to know that I have decided not to make the play before the next General Election. I don't think it matters missing the fifth anniversary next spring; I am sure, though, that your work would be greatly compromised if it got caught up in a pre-election frenzy – and I do believe we will have an election next year!
Yours ever, Alasdair.

Coln St Aldwyns, Gloucestershire. 2 August 1986
Dear Alasdair

I've been away on family holiday in Ireland, so have only just seen your letter of July 21st about the cancellation of the present production of *The Falklands Play*, because of the next election.

I am disturbed by this. It would be a great kindness were you to set my mind at rest over these points:

1. On June 2nd I asked you what your position would be were an election called. You replied that it would not matter; the earliest that could happen, barring a national catastrophe, was autumn 1987. Transmission on April 2nd would therefore not be affected.

   Apart from newspaper speculation during the silly season, what has happened so radically to alter your view?
2. Would you, in 1950, have cancelled a specially-commissioned, three-hour play celebrating the nation's winning the War over another aggressor, in case it influenced voters in a 1951 election?
3. Could the BBC not have demonstrated its impartiality by proceeding with the present production – perhaps you have not been fully briefed on how far it had got, and what a strong team was assembling – but postponing transmission were an election called?
4. By its very nature, *The Falklands Play* is pro-Government and pro-Mrs Thatcher. You personally commissioned it. It is meticulously researched.

   As you have cancelled it apparently for fear it might influence voters, have you also cancelled other programmes, however accurate, containing *anti*-Government and *anti*-Mrs Thatcher arguments, lest they influence voters the other way?
5. Since the next election is given as the reason for cancellation, can you assure me that a new production will be mounted after that election?

6. [A detailed account of Peter Goodchild's visit to my house on July 7th, his 'suggestions' for political changes to the script, his subsequent letter saying these were mandatory or the production would be cancelled, my refusal to comply without evidence, the cancellation of the production within a week] ... Was this simple coincidence?
7. For reasons you are aware of, I am now bearing a very considerable financial loss over *The Falklands Play*. I am certain the BBC will act honourably over this.
8. As a result of over 80 plays and series transmitted over twenty years, I've become known as the only television playwright of the first rank [in this country] with beliefs right of centre. You yourself were good enough to say that my plays 'enrich the BBC'.

   The fact is, however, that the BBC has now consistently blocked my plays for over five years, giving reasons which, for the most part, I find puzzling. I attach details of another recent example.

   Fortunately, ITV continues to produce them, obtaining high viewing figures which must indicate a good audience appetite for them.

   Surely I would be less than human if I did not see the BBC's action over *The Falklands Play* as yet another example of the same thing?

As you know, the Attorney General had agreed to the BBC's request to read the play. As a matter of courtesy, and to protect my own position, I shall have to let him know that truth and accuracy are not the grounds on which the present production has been cancelled.

I have, incidentally, now received some purely technical corrections from the Ministry of Defence and other Government departments, which I will incorporate into the final, rehearsal, draft. I shall also copy this letter to Hutchinsons, who are publishing the play.

Your comments on the points I've listed above would be very much appreciated.

Yours sincerely, Ian.

The other 'recent example' was *BB and Joe* (see page 21).

The reference to the Attorney General was the result of Peter Goodchild's request to me on July 7, that I should approach one or two people at the political centre of the Falklands conflict for their comments on the general verisimilitude of the script. I pointed out that such a request should surely come openly from the BBC itself, but he said it was better to channel the *request* unofficially through me. If I obtained agreement, the BBC would send the script.

I approached Sir Michael Havers, obtained his agreement, and wrote to Peter Goodchild on July 17 to say so, giving Sir Michael's address. But Goodchild never followed it up.

Alasdair Milne's reply to my eight detailed questions was as follows:

Broadcasting House, London. 8 August 1986
Dear Ian

Many thanks for your letter of August 2nd.

You appear to see something sinister in my decision. As you know, I thought very well of the play, and still do. Others at the Television Centre have reservations, but it is my hope that we will produce the play when the election is out of the way.

I did not know that the BBC had 'consistently blocked your plays for over five years'. Indeed, I am very sorry to hear it because I certainly believe that your work has enriched the BBC. I sincerely hope that your relationship with the BBC will continue to be a good one.

Yours sincerely, Alasdair.

Coln St Aldwyns, Gloucestershire. 12 August 1986.
Dear Alasdair

Many thanks for your letter of August 8th.

The 'reservations' held by some at Television Centre were put to me. I refused to comply with those that were flatly untrue, and for which they could offer no evidence. The production was then cancelled.

I, too, earnestly wish for a good relationship with the BBC.

Yours sincerely, Ian.

Several people suggested I should release the story to the press. I was certain this would be a mistake. Once such a matter explodes in public, everyone digs himself into an entrenched position, *amour propre* becomes involved. It would have become ten times more difficult to achieve my object, of getting the play back into the schedules.

The right course, I felt, was through the Governors. The

weakness in Milne, Cotton and Grade's case was surely that they had taken a key *policy* decision with many implications – to start cancelling major programmes on the grounds of a coming election, long before that election was declared. Policy is the prerogative of the Governors, the central duty laid upon them by the Crown. Management is there to carry it out, not decide it.

So I began to compile a dossier of the case for the Chairman, Stuart Young, the key correspondence, the key dates, contracts and production documents. If it was of cast-iron accuracy, then it would speak for itself. I was again commuting, this time to Frankfurt and Mainz, writing a play for German ZDF Television. And just as I completed the dossier, Stuart Young died.

Three days later, the BBC began to transmit Alan Bleasdale's four-part drama series *The Monocled Mutineer*. There was an immediate and angry public outcry at what was seen as a grossly left-wing distortion of the Etaples Mutiny of 1917. The historical consultant to the programme said it was 'riddled with errors' and a 'tissue of lies'.

The *Daily Mail* later weighed in with a two-page spread exposing the BBC's claim that it was 'an enthralling, true-life story' – the Corporation had taken highly expensive, full-page advertisements in the national press to say so – by listing the entirely invented, unhistorical, politically loaded events that appeared in the plays, advertised as The Truth.

Its leader said,

'The report on these pages, exposing the dishonesty of the BBC in advertising their *Monocled Mutineer* series as a true story, shows exactly to what depths of cynicism and irresponsibility the BBC has sunk.

'That a segment of British history has been twisted and fictionalised from a Leftwing viewpoint may not be too surprising. Many people believe that the BBC is engaged in a long-term operation to rewrite history, because of its hatred of our Imperial past.

'Unfortunately, it is often successful, and there will be many young people who will now accept at face value the myth of Percy Toplis as a working class revolutionary dedicated to overthrowing a widely-hated, aristocratic establishment . . .'

Bill Cotton was stung by these comments into a vigorous public defence. He berated us all for not realizing that when the BBC said that something was a 'true-life story', they did not mean it had actually *happened*.

He fulminated that the series represented not the truth about the Etaples Mutiny (which most viewers, in their innocence, thought it did – including this viewer) but 'the *greater* truth . . . about the First World War. I stand by its integrity'. And those hugely expensive, full-page advertisements, saying something rather different? No comment.

The press began to debate whether the BBC needed a 'consensus-chairman', which the Home Secretary was said to favour, or a tough guy, which the Prime Minister was reputed to prefer. Certainly the latter was more likely to use a case like *The Falklands Play* as a means of asserting his authority over management on his arrival. I began to think ahead along those lines.

On September 19 I heard that Norris McWhirter was taking action on my behalf and intended to publish the story. I had never met or spoken to him, though I knew that he had several times in the past fought some notable cases on behalf of individuals against bull-headed bureaucracies, with great success. But on this occasion, I thought, he must be discouraged.

I eventually tracked him down via his old Who's Who number. He had been trying to get through to me, without success (we are ex-directory).

He told me his plans to publish; I told him my objections. But he argued that the case had far wider implications than I was taking into account. The Chairman was in the process of selection. The BBC was at a crossroads. The public must know what is really happening within the Corporation, what problems there really are, or how can such a crucial appointment be made effectively?

Of course he was right. But he only had half the story. I posted him the entire dossier, dates, letters, all documentation, with my blessing, sat back, and waited.

On Monday September 29, Norris published the story on the front page of *Free Nation*, the journal of the Freedom Association. Copies of this and a four-page press release were taken by car round to all major London newspapers at 10.30 a.m.

From this moment, the two telephone lines to this house never stopped ringing. As I put either receiver down, it immediately began to ring again, 8 a.m. to 9 p.m. I gave 84 interviews in four days, until I was hoarse – often the same journalist coming back to check his story again and again. I was determined that the press would get the facts absolutely clear.

The *Evening Standard* gave full, front-page, headline coverage, the major story of the day. Next morning all the nationals carried it, some with substantial coverage. The interest was intense; here was a well-documented case of attempted political loading of a major BBC programme, which had been cancelled only when I refused to comply.

Moreover, besides *The Queen's Arms*, Fleet Street had discovered another BBC Falklands play in early production – *Tumbledown*, by Charles Wood, which they said had an emotive anti-Mrs-Thatcher's-Government theme. It was said that Michael Grade had abandoned the normal budget ceiling of £390,000 per screen hour for this play, which is rare. And the coup de grace was this: production was scheduled for January, and transmission in October 1987 – one of the hot dates for the General Election.

One telephone call that extraordinary September 30 was most welcome. Sir John Woolf, of Anglia Television and Romulus Films, producer of *The Day of the Jackal*, *Oliver*, *Room at the Top* and many other award-winning films, rang me. He is an old friend and has produced plays of mine on ITV in the past.

He said he had read the press, and, from the sound of it,

would very much like to produce the play. He sent a car to collect a copy of the script.

The following morning he rang again, to say (a) he had read it, liked it enormously, and wished to confirm how much he'd like to produce it on ITV; but (b) Michael Grade had rung Anglia Television at the highest possible level, having read of their interest in the press. He said that no way was he going to allow the BBC to release the remaining 17 months' copyright licence they held on the play. He told Anglia, however, 'This call is not for the press.'

Woolf himself had already talked to Fleet Street about his wish to go ahead with production. In view of Grade's telephone call and his insistence that the press was not to be informed, he told me he now felt in a most foolish position.

A few days later, Cedric Messina's agent rang the Head of Plays at Anglia, John Rosenberg, who confirmed this. Thus the BBC had blocked the play themselves, and actively prevented ITV from producing it. If that isn't gagging, what is?

Three times, on the day the story broke in the national press, Peter Goodchild rang Cedric Messina at his home, in a state of considerable agitation. He was seeking general agreement for a press statement that the real reason for cancellation had been the escalation of production costs – a hopeless hypothesis, as budgeting had been so recent.

In all three calls, he reminded Messina that he was under BBC contract [to produce *The Falklands Play*] and therefore absolutely forbidden to speak to the press. Later that day, without consulting a single programme-maker concerned, and in particular having muzzled Messina from public comment, the BBC issued two press statements about the cancelled production, which shocked producer, director, myself and many in Plays Department who had been concerned with it, by its bald untruthfulness. The first was issued by the BBC Press Office.

> 'A statement by Bill Cotton, Managing Director, BBC-tv.
>
> 'Ian Curteis completed the first draft of his *Falklands Play* three

and a half years after we had commissioned it. In July we postponed the making of it for the following reasons:

'In our professional opinion, it is not a completed commission. Following a meeting with me, Peter Goodchild, Head of Television Plays, saw Mr Curteis to discuss the strengths and weaknesses of his first draft. After a meeting in Mr Curteis's home the author set out the main points in a letter to Mr Goodchild dated July 8th and raised no objections to Mr Goodchild's observations about his script.

'It would be irresponsible of the BBC at a time when the country is leading up to an election to embark on a play portraying a Prime Minister in office, other serving ministers and MPs. At such a sensitive time, all political sides would be entitled to take issue with us not only on the script but the direction and even the choice of actors. It would have been an improper project for the BBC to undertake and potentially damaging to the producer and performers it employs. I can understand Mr Curteis's disappointment that the production of his play had to be postponed, but the BBC cannot be stampeded into investing a great deal of money into a production when it feels uneasy on such major counts.

'The BBC utterly refutes any suggestion that it has postponed this play for any other reason.

'It also refutes the allegation that Peter Goodchild went to see the author to alter the political slant of the play – an absurd proposition at any time. He went as part of the normal process of developing a script from its first to second draft.'

The second statement issued through the Press Association, quoted a BBC spokesman thus:

'The BBC had creative discussions about Ian Curteis's draft script. This kind of dialogue between producer and writer is a matter of routine in any major drama production. No bookings had been made for studio time. It was far too early for this to be done. There had been no commitment to the production of this play.'

These two statements present an astonishing mixture of innuendo, revelation and straight untruths.

BBC claim: That the meeting on July 7 was a routine 'creative discussion' between producer and author.

Comment: The producer – the highly experienced BBC officer responsible – was not present. He had already rejected the proposed changes as improper, irresponsible, political, unhistorical and unjustified. The Head of Plays had no *locus standi*.

BBC claim: The script was 3½ years in delivery.

Comment: Innuendo. The BBC had agreed to the postponement, the reason for which it itself had been responsible for. This had been cleared by the then Head of Plays, the Producer, and later confirmed to the Director General. The BBC were fully aware of it.

BBC claim: It was a first draft.

Comment: It was the fourth draft. On January 19 1986, I had written to Peter Goodchild that I was then on the third draft. On July 7, he had gone through all the earlier drafts, in detail, with his own hands.

BBC claim: 'In our professional opinion, it is not a completed commission.'

Comment: The BBC Copyright and Contract Department had formally accepted the fourth draft, in the full legal and contractual sense, in writing, following instructions from Plays Department to do so, on April 29. This was subject only to any comments the producer and director may have – a normal caveat I was happy to comply with.

Bill Cotton has no professional experience whatever, that I am aware of, of writing, producing or directing a serious play. The *professionals* concerned were unanimous in their opinion of the text; they are among the most experienced in British television:

Alasdair Milne, former Director General of the BBC: 'I have now read *The Falklands Play*, and it makes a terrific story . . . I thought very highly of the play, and still do . . . Your work has enriched the BBC.'

Sir John Woolf, of Anglia Television and Romulus Films, producer of *Room at the Top*, *Oliver*, *The Day of the Jackal*: 'I liked the play enormously, and only wish we could have produced it on ITV.'

Cedric Messina, doyen of BBC drama producers, founder-producer BBC Shakespeare series, for ten years producer BBC Play of the Month: 'It is a very fine play and should be produced.'

David Giles, senior BBC Classic Serial director, director *The Forsyte Saga*, *The Mayor of Casterbridge*, *The Barchester Chronicles*, etc: 'The fact that has got lost in all the mayhem is just what a splendid play it is . . . it is spellbinding.'

BBC claim: That it would be irresponsible of the BBC to produce such a play at this time.

Comment: When Bill Cotton sent Peter Goodchild to see me on July 7, clearly there was no objection of that sort. Why else would Goodchild have taken so much trouble over suggested changes to the script?

Fourteen days later, on July 21, when I had refused to make these politically loading changes without evidence or explanation, it had suddenly become 'irresponsible . . . an improper project . . . the BBC cannot be stampeded'.

BBC claim: The changes required were not political.

Comment: Their *effect* would have been highly political. As the author, I would have had to take full legal responsibility for such alterations; and under the 'warranty' clause of my contract of licence, would have been responsible for the BBC's costs as well as my own, had any of the Ministers of the Crown who would undoubtedly have been libelled, chosen to sue.

BBC claim: My letter of July 8 did not object to the proposed changes.

Comment: Readers will recall the context of that holding letter. The changes were then only 'ideas for me to think about, – ponder over'. When they became mandatory, I objected strenuously.

BBC claim: There had been no commitment to the production of the play.

Comment: The BBC's largest studio had been booked Jan 24–Feb 8; the producer had signed his contract; the budget had been completed and authorised; transmission on April 2 had been confirmed.

The most interesting revelation is Bill Cotton's clear statement that the planned meeting between him and Goodchild *had* taken place, immediately before the latter came down to see me. Goodchild had insisted to me that it hadn't happened, as Cotton had cut it to go off to Wimbledon.

Why should Goodchild have attempted to hide the fact that the meeting had taken place? The only explanation I can think of is that *the proposed changes actually came from Cotton*, using Goodchild as messenger. Goodchild himself was always unable to explain or support them, by evidence or argument.

If this is the case – and I earnestly hope it is not, and that the BBC can come up with a better explanation – then we have an interesting situation. If this attempt, using a front-man, to insert unhistorical, politically-slanting material into a major programme failed, and has been exposed, how many other times has it happened successfully?

I was unprepared for the public reaction that followed. Scores of letters poured into my house, mostly from complete strangers. All were heartwarmingly congratulatory. It was clear that the affair had touched a nerve, given a focus to a vast number of people who knew there was something deeply wrong within the BBC, but who could never work out *how* such things could happen.

The subject kept popping up at the Conservative Party conference in September, in both the main and fringe sessions, and later in the House of Commons. A friend mentioned there had been a Question to the Prime Minister about it; I bought Hansard, and there first read the name of the splendid Richard Holt, MP for Langbaurgh, who had been battling to get the facts publicly established. I rang him, we met, I passed over copies of all the correspondence and the script. He battled harder.

Every time I read of a public figure commenting on the affair,

I Xeroxed yet another fat bundle of the key papers and correspondence, and posted them – to forty or fifty people. The affair was raised a further five times in the House of Commons. It cropped up in Robin Day's Question Time on BBC-1, and on Channel Four's A Week in Politics. Friends wrote from Berlin, Hong Kong and Johannesburg to say they had heard about it on the wireless – ironically on BBC World Service. I was asked to address a combined meeting of the Conservative Backbench Home Affairs and Media committees at the House of Commons, on political bias in television drama generally: much of the 45 minutes of questions that followed probed closely into exactly what had happened over *The Falklands Play*. The press kept rumbling on about it.

Vociferous public comment continued about the other Falklands play going through the BBC Plays Department – *Tumbledown*, by Charles Wood, produced by Richard Broke, the producer of *The Monocled Mutineer*. The author talked about his play to Corinna Honan of the *Daily Mail*:

> 'It has a deep political message that war is futile. The subversive message is think twice before you elect to serve in an army . . . Is it right to ask people to die, particularly for something like the Falklands? It didn't seem right to me . . . I want people to start questioning what it is we did . . .'

Criticism became louder. If a pro-British Falklands Play was too sensitive a subject before an election, ran the argument, what about one like that? And what about the unusual lifting of the budget ceiling? And the projected transmission date?

After three weeks of such pressure, Peter Goodchild announced to the press on October 27 that *Tumbledown* had been postponed. 'Not for political reasons,' he insisted, 'purely a question of budget' – the selfsame reason he had tried so hard to get agreement on behind the scenes, when *The Falklands Play* was cancelled.

Meantime, there had been a sharp change of direction in the BBC. Members of the Board of Management started to put it about that the real reason for cancellation was not the reason the Director General had given – the proximity of an election – but that it was a truly dreadful script.

I first heard of this happening at the BBC's reception during the Conservative Party conference at Bournemouth. Ivan Lawrence, QC, MP, and Miss Moulin of Policy Research Associates, asked Peter Ibbotson exactly why *The Falklands Play* had been cancelled. Ibbotson is Michael Grade's Chief of Staff; his name may be better known as a former Producer of Panorama, and chief defendant in the recent High Court trial when the BBC finally admitted it had libelled two MPs by trying to brand them publicly as neo-Nazis. This had cost the taxpayer £500,000.

'Quite simple,' Ibbotson replied, 'it's a terrible play.' The characters were two-dimensional, it was just bad. '*That*'s why we tried to alter it – to improve it as a play.' Brian Wenham joined them. He had recently been translated from Director of Programmes, Television, to Managing Director, BBC Radio, and must therefore have been party to the earlier history of *The Falklands Play*. On being told the subject under discussion, he began enthusiastically to agree with Ibbotson. This, then, had become the party line.

Then there was the press conference called by Michael Grade in his office at Television Centre on October 2 – but only to selected journalists. I know of at least three other, properly accredited, NUJ-card-carrying, reputable Fleet Street journalists who could not obtain entry.

As those who were allowed to attend were entering Grade's office, Cotton was leaving, very much in casual clothes, smiling and nodding to them on his way out. Goodchild was also present. I have a transcript and newspaper report of what was then said.

Grade spent nearly all the conference pointing out that the real reason for cancellation was not the election, but the laughably poor quality of the script. 'There was absolutely no commitment to production or transmission on this project,' he said. 'I respect the Prime Minister. All the alterations we proposed to Curteis had been *to protect Mrs Thatcher*!'

It all so reminded me of a joke we used to tell at my little village Council school. A thoroughly shifty second-hand car salesman had come up with an entirely new alibi on the second day of his trial.

'But that wasn't the story you told me yesterday!' remarked the Judge. 'No!' replied Shifty, wide-eyed with *chutzpah*, 'but you didn't believe that one, did you?'

As soon as Duke Hussey was appointed as Chairman of the BBC, I was in correspondence with him and Lord Barnett, the Vice-Chairman. After apparently putting their heads together, they both wrote to say they had passed the matter down to Alasdair Milne to deal with.

Then followed a second exchange of letters between Milne and myself, of which I give extracts:

From Milne to Curteis, November 3 1986.

'... I cannot, I'm afraid, accept your proposal to go ahead with production but delay showing the play until after the election. I do not want to tie up money in a programme that would have to sit on the shelf for some time ...'

This was the only time the Director General had answered the often-asked question: why not proceed to recording the play, but delay transmission until after the election?

His explanation is not, alas, borne out by the facts. It is common practice to record a play – often a high-budget one – but delay transmission for a year or more for perfectly normal, routine reasons of scheduling. I could name half-a-dozen recent examples.

From Curteis to Milne, November 5 1986.

'... I hope you will see from these examples [of the BBC's contradictory statements] that you and the Governors are being told a good deal less than the truth. Many people in Plays Department are fully aware of what actually happened, and the ineffective attempt to cover it up ...'

From Milne to Curteis, November 11 1986.

'. . . The Director of Programmes [Michael Grade] has told me that certainly the production was pencilled in . . . he is the ultimate arbiter.'

From Curteis to Milne, November 13 1986.

'I was surprised to read . . . that Michael Grade is the ultimate arbiter in this matter. Are not you Director General? Did you not personally commission this play, and express warm approval of it to me, in writing, when you read it? Did you not assure me, on June 2, that an election would not affect production?'

From Milne to Curteis, November 14 1986.

'As to the question of the election affecting production, I have reminded you several times that when we met in June, *I had not even read your play* . . . [my emphasis] . . . You continue to insist that my staff have been guilty of dubious political machinations. I continue to insist that this is nonsense.'

From Curteis to Milne, November 16 1986.

'Three weeks before we met in June, you wrote to me " . . . I am reading the play at the moment". A copy of this letter is attached.

'I am therefore unsure how to take your new claim, that you had *not* read it when we met, and you assured me that an election would not affect production.

'You also say "I have reminded you several times" that, when we met in June, you had not read the play. This claim is entirely new to me. Perhaps you would kindly indicate the letters you are referring to?

'No, I have never insisted that your staff has been guilty of dubious political machinations. I do suggest that two of them have been guilty of abuse of public power. The majority of your staff, who are most loyal to the spirit of the Charter, are well aware of what actually happened; they were shocked by the BBC's statements to the press, which they knew were untrue.

'I once more urge you and the Chairman to set up an objective enquiry to establish the facts. This matter is not going to go away . . .'

From Milne to Curteis, November 20 1986.

'I was indeed reading the play when I wrote [on May 14]; when we met, [on June 2] I had actually read six pages . . . I have no intention of setting up an enquiry. I am perfectly well aware of the facts. And I do wish we could rest this correspondence . . .'

From Curteis to Milne, November 26 1986.

'I, too, wish we could rest this correspondence. Had you only answered the simple questions I believe I have every right to ask, it would have come to a natural conclusion long ago.

'Those eight questions are, essentially, set out in my first letter to you after the production was cancelled [August 2nd] . . . In spite of my requests, you have only ever answered one of them. The rest you have simply ignored.

'I invite you, once more, to answer those questions. I have tried to make them very clear and exact; I am certain you would wish to reply with similar clarity and detail.

'As you assure me no enquiry is needed since you are perfectly well aware of the facts, I am sure this will present no difficulties.

'Meantime, I note from our latest exchange that (a) you were "reading the play at the moment" on May 14, (b) three weeks later, on June 2nd, you had read six pages (out of 198), and (c) it was on that basis that you could assure me an election would not affect production.'

There was a further exchange between us which added nothing new, except this point:

From Milne to Curteis, December 16 1986.

'I understand that you are suggesting that our correspondence will be published with the play. Are you seeking my permission for this?'

From Curteis to Milne, December 20 1986.

'Certainly I would normally seek the BBC's permission to publish its letters, for copyright reasons and out of common courtesy. However, as the BBC published *my* letters without seeking permission (*Daily Telegraph*, October 2) could you explain the Corporation's ethical standards over such matters?'

I received a printed card of acknowledgement, saying a reply would be sent in due course. Five weeks of silence followed.

On January 29, Hussey and Barnett summoned Milne and offered him the choice of resignation or being sacked. He chose resignation. It is said to have been a very brief meeting.

On February 8 and 15, the *Sunday Telegraph* published an abridgement of this introduction, giving it substantial coverage. A few days before, a copy of the complete text had been delivered to Peter Goodchild.

He wrote to the newspaper, officially, on BBC letterhead, complaining of the 'grave and wounding' nature of the articles, but took none of the legal options open to him to prevent publication, had he grounds for doing so.

Public and press reaction to the abridgement was immediate. The affair was again raised in the House of Commons. The *Daily Express* called it 'a revelation of deception, bias, low professional standards and half-truths'. Paul Johnson wrote, in the *Spectator*:

> 'Curteis's account exposes the shoddy way the BBC is run nowadays: its mendacity, hypocrisy and duplicity, as well as its obvious political bias. Some of the most senior officials at the BBC were involved in this sorry tale, and if they are in a position to challenge Curteis's allegations, they have an obvious legal remedy. One of the BBC's fictions – that the Corporation could not transmit such a programme in a likely election year – has already been exposed by its own decision to show in June a tendentious version of the Profumo affair calculated to damage the Conservative Party. But the BBC takes falsehood in its stride these days . . .'

The BBC immediately requested the *Sunday Telegraph* to reserve a 2000-word space the following Sunday, for Peter Goodchild to reply. The newspaper agreed, and awaited the copy.

Goodchild wrote his 2000 words, and submitted them to his superiors for their approval. On Thursday February 19 the *Sunday Telegraph* was informed that he would not after all be sending his piece for publication. Bill Cotton would be writing a 400-word letter instead.

That letter was delivered by hand on Friday 20, and published by the *Sunday Telegraph* on the 22nd. The 1600 word space abruptly left blank was filled by the newspaper with a profile of Bill Cotton, which pointed out his absence of experience, qualifications or judgement in any area outside Light Entertainment.

It also quoted the opinion of one of his senior colleagues, concerning one reason why Cotton may have overruled the highly experienced professionals in Plays Department to cancel *The Falklands Play*: 'He was damned if he was going to allow Mrs Thatcher to get the credit for the Falklands all over again.'

Cotton's letter read:

'Ian Curteis's two long articles in the *Sunday Telegraph* seek to prove that the BBC, for dubious motives, sought improperly to prevent the production of his play about the Falklands War. The allegation is both ill-founded and also extremely damaging to the BBC. It is also damaging to Alasdair Milne, Peter Goodchild and myself.

'Alasdair, I am sure, will speak for himself if he chooses. For myself I find ridiculous Mr Curteis' assertions that I dispatched Mr Goodchild to coerce him into changing the political point of view of his play.

'It is equally ridiculous to state that Mr Goodchild's conversations were politically rather than professionally motivated. (I would remind Mr Curteis that Mr Goodchild's professional ability has won his drama productions international recognition and many awards). BBC Television produces 60 plays every year, but has at any one time up to four times that number of scripts in development. Many of them are delayed, or cancelled. Such is the nature of drama production.

'In the case of *The Falklands Play*, it was referred to Director of Programmes, Michael Grade, and myself, to read in July 1986. It was the first draft script seen by the BBC. We separately concluded that the script was, *as a drama*, not yet good enough for the investment of the £1 million necessary to finance such a production. That was a proper professional decision, one of the dozens made each year in assessing the potential, readiness and cost of major drama projects.

'Subsequently the Director-General took the decision that in any event it would be unwise to enter into the production of the play in the period running up to the next General Election. This was endorsed by the BBC Board of Governors. The delay since commissioning the project in 1983 had placed us within that period and there was due concern about the problems of portraying active leading politicians at this time. (Contrary to Mr Curteis's assertion, it was also agreed at this time that the BBC would release the rights to a third party if there was an offer for them. To date there has not been one.)

Both these decisions, the one professional as to the quality of the script, the other with due regard to the public interest in a sensitive political period, were properly and carefully made. There has been no censorship and no conspiracy.

'Bill Cotton, Managing Director, Television, BBC.

The *Sunday Telegraph* rang me for my comments. I replied:

(a) I do not attack the BBC; I offer hard evidence concerning five of its employees out of 28,000.
(b) My articles were precise, specific and factual; Mr Cotton has replied in the most general and unsupported terms.
(c) If Mr Cotton and Mr Grade thought the play so poor, why were studios booked, producer signed up, budget finalised and approved, transmission dates fixed? Why was I asked to incorporate political points I knew were untrue, if the script was unacceptable anyway?
(d) Mr Goodchild's awards were all for scientific programmes in his previous appointment. He has won no awards as Head of Plays.
(e) Of course no third party has made an offer for the play. Anglia TV wished to do so, but Michael Grade telephoned them at the highest possible level on 30 September 1986 to say that the BBC would not release the rights.

Politically, I am a moderate, and the play reflects the straight-down-the-centre line and sense of history that the great majority of the British felt and believed during the crisis. Numerous public opinion polls testify to this. What we achieved then, and its repercussions since, justify pride and celebration.

With this in mind, I believe these to be the unanswered questions:

1. Of course I accept that such a play as this presents peculiar problems of sensitivity before a General Election. That is obvious.

   However: no such problems were present when Peter Goodchild asked for politically loading changes on July 7, following his meeting with Bill Cotton. Why else travel down to Gloucestershire with such a well-worked-out plan for altering the script?

   Fourteen days later, when I had refused to make such changes without evidence, it had suddenly become 'irresponsible . . . the country is leading up to a general election . . . improper' – and cancelled.

   What happened, politically, during those fourteen sleepy summer days, so radically to alter the BBC's prognosis of a General Election?

2. Had I complied, would the production have proceeded?

3. What was the 'watershed date' during July 1986, when the BBC decided to start cancelling programmes because an election was improperly close? Who made this decision? On what evidence? What other programmes were cancelled at that time for that reason?

4. Why were none of the programme makers consulted, and why was the producer specifically muzzled from providing factual evidence, before the BBC issued its untruthful and misleading press statements of September 30 1986?

5. Why, with a definite approach from ITV, did Michael Grade telephone Anglia TV and say he had no intention of releasing the BBC's remaining rights? If, as he told the press, the script was 'laughably poor', why did he not leap at the chance to get rid of it? Why did he not want the press to know about his call?

6. The BBC's duty to be impartial has never applied to

individual plays in the same way that it does to, say, news or current affairs programmes. If it had, the Corporation would be unable to transmit most of the world's great plays.

Impartiality is interpreted as it relates to drama as a rough balance of plays over a period. Yet there are many, including myself, who feel that the thrust of nearly all new plays on the BBC – 95% of which are actively commissioned by the Corporation – are very markedly towards one end only of the political spectrum.

How, in practice, does the BBC endeavour to fulfill its obligations over this point?

7. Was the real reason for not proceeding to the scheduled recording of *The Falklands Play* and *then* deciding whether or not the election was improperly close for transmission, as follows:

In the *Real Lives* case, the weakness of the Board of Management's position was that the programme had already been recorded. It then fell to the Governors, as constitutionally it should, to view the film and make the policy decision whether or not to transmit.

According to Michael Leapman's *The Last Days of the Beeb*, Bill Cotton 'passionately' resisted their doing this, but was overruled.

If *The Falklands Play* had also been recorded, was there not a risk that the same situation could happen again? – and that the one thing the Board of Management fear most, would be brought to pass – that the Governors should be allowed to govern?

Coln St Aldwyns I.C.
Gloucestershire
February 1987

THE FALKLANDS PLAY

PART ONE

1. LIBRARY FILM

A passenger plane seen high up, a silver speck in the sky. Creep in the sounds of the House of Commons.

SPEAKER (*voice over*): Order, order. Mr Nicholas Ridley.

RIDLEY (*voice over*): With permission, Mr Speaker, I wish to make a statement on the Falkland Islands.

2. INT. THE PLANE

NICHOLAS RIDLEY *(fifty-three), Minister of State at the Foreign Office, in shirt-sleeves in a curtained-off section of the first-class compartment. He is at the end of a twelve-hour flight from Buenos Aires, and looks tired and dishevelled. He is drafting a speech, silver pencil on pad.*

RIDLEY (*voice over*): I have this morning returned from consulting the islanders as to the future of their homeland. We have no doubt whatever about British sovereignty over the Islands. The Argentines, however, are being far more urgent in their demands and insistence on ownership. This dispute has continued for over a century. Decisive action *must* be taken . . .

ROBIN FEARN *(forty-five), head of the South American Department at the Foreign Office, leans over.*

FEARN: Heathrow in forty minutes. (RIDLEY *grunts.*) You're not going straight to the House of Commons?

RIDLEY: (*blinking back tiredness*) We've got to stop the rumours.

FEARN: Why don't you get some sleep?

RIDLEY: I'm all right. Oh – we'll check this with Peter Carrington on the way through.

(*He stares at what he has written.*)

RIDLEY (*voice over*): The options available to us include surrendering sovereignty of the islands to the Argentines, in exchange for a long lease of them back to Her Majesty's Government – *leaseback*.

3. INT. THE FOREIGN SECRETARY'S ROOM, FOREIGN OFFICE

The grand, lofty room of so much history. Full-length windows in two walls overlook St James's Park and Horseguards. The Foreign Secretary, LORD CARRINGTON *(sixty-three), stands at the long table, which is stacked with reports and red cabinet boxes. He is brusque and vigorous. He holds up* RIDLEY'S *draft with some amazement.*

CARRINGTON: And you seriously intend to announce this, in half an hour?

RIDLEY: I've toned that draft down a bit.

CARRINGTON: The back-benchers will fall on you like wolves! They're rubbed sore enough as it is, over Rhodesia – I mean, Zimbabwe. What do you think, Robin?

FEARN: If Mr Ridley can crack the Falklands problem once for all, everyone will applaud.

CARRINGTON: Well of course, of course they will! But *this*? (*He throws the draft down onto the table and crosses over to them.*) It's not that it's wrong in principle. It's far too blunt! And the timing's all wrong. Can't you put it on ice until Rhodesia's out of the way? – er, I mean, Zimbabwe's out of the way?

RIDLEY: Peter, we just can't *afford* to keep the islands on indefinitely!

FEARN: Foreign Secretary, the telephones from Port Stanley have been red hot ever since we left, with the wildest rumours about what we're cooking up. A statement *has* to be made.

CARRINGTON: Well, I'd sooner face a herd of charging rhino.

4. INT. HOUSE OF COMMONS

RIDLEY *is concluding his statement at the despatch box. He hides his jet-lag by a performance of crispness and decision.*

RIDLEY: . . . It is absolutely essential, however, that British law, administration and way of life continue on the islands for the time being. (*emphatically*) That is what the islanders have chosen, and that is what they shall have.

He sits. A rising hum of disturbed comment from both sides of the house. PETER SHORE *rises, pushing back a lock of hair from his forehead.*

SPEAKER: Mr Peter Shore.

SHORE: This is a very worrying statement. (*Shouts of hear, hear! from both sides of the House.*) Will the Minister confirm that involved here are the rights and future of one thousand eight hundred British people in a territory that was originally uninhabited? Will he confirm that there is – (*thumping the despatch box*) – *no question whatever* of surrendering these islands to Argentina, against their wishes? (*Roars of agreement from both sides.* RIDLEY *was expecting opposition, but is visibly taken aback by such collective vehemence.*) Such wishes are not simply *advice* to the British Government. Surely they are of paramount importance! Has that been made absolutely clear to the Argentines?

He sits. RIDLEY *rises.*

RIDLEY: The answer to all the Right Honourable gentleman's questions, is 'Yes'.

SPEAKER: Mr Russell Johnston.

JOHNSTON: Is the Minister aware that there is no support whatever in this House for shameful schemes to get rid of these islands, that have been festering in the Foreign Office for years?

Roars of agreement all round.

RIDLEY (*rising*): Perhaps I am more aware of what the *islanders* think about this matter than the Honourable gentleman is.

This reply is greeted by some derision and a rising hubbub of comment. Several members are on their feet, trying to catch the Speaker's eye. The speed with which the House has gone from silence to angry rumpus is a measure of how close to the surface this matter was simmering. The Speaker is heard vainly calling for order. RIDLEY *is pale, and visibly shaking.*

SPEAKER (*behind noise*): Mr David Lambie.

LAMBIE: Is the Minister aware that there was no need for his statement today, which will only increase the islanders' suspicions about our intentions? (*almost shouting*) Why can't you leave well alone?!

Close shot RIDLEY, *as he rises and shouts into the din, with exasperation.*

RIDLEY: If we don't do something, Argentina will invade! And there would be nothing whatever we could do about it!

5. INT. THE PRIME MINISTER'S STUDY, 10 DOWNING STREET

A light and airy room containing a ring of armchairs by the fireplace and the PM's desk. It is her normal, daily place of work. CARRINGTON, *red cabinet box in hand, is waiting to take her down to a Cabinet meeting.*

CARRINGTON: The poor fellow took a terrible hammering. It was as if some sort of floodgates burst.

PM'S VOICE (*through open door to inner sanctum*): Well, are you surprised? His timing was totally and utterly wrong, Peter, totally and utterly wrong! (*The* PM *appears. She is fifty-seven, vigorous, immaculately fresh and well-groomed.*) Even to consider just handing over two thousand of our own people to an evil regime like that! – their record on human rights is blood-curdling!

She starts gathering her own papers into her cabinet box.

CARRINGTON: In return for a long leaseback –

PM (*cutting him off*): Which the Argentines would instantly dishonour. The whole thing smacks to me of a nasty little Foreign Office plot.

CARRINGTON: Margaret, I don't really –

PM: They've been trying to rid themselves of those islands ever since I've been in Parliament!

CARRINGTON (*quite sharply*): Well, that's hardly surprising, is it? We can't *afford* to keep them on.

PM: I don't mean you, dear.

CARRINGTON (*as they go*): Eight thousand miles away – a contracting navy – in two year's time we won't even be able to defend them! . . .

6. INT. THE STAIRCASE AND ANTE-ROOM TO THE CABINET ROOM, 10 DOWNING STREET

The PM *and* CARRINGTON *descend briskly, passing the long, double-banked line of portraits of former prime ministers, ranged down one side.*

PM: Why can't we simply leave things as they are?

CARRINGTON: Because the current stalemate is producing economic stagnation. But if we do nothing, Nicholas thinks they could invade.

PM (*stopping*): What?

CARRINGTON: He says there's a new mood in Buenos Aires.

PM: More realistic?

CARRINGTON: More hotheaded.

PM: Hm. (*she steps off again.*) They've been talking about invasion for years.

CARRINGTON (*insisting*): Nicholas has been there, and we haven't!

They come to the ante-room outside the Cabinet Room. Members of the full Cabinet sit on the table or chairs or stand about chatting, their red or black despatch boxes in hand.

PM: Good morning, good morning everyone! What a lovely morning, the frost looks simply magical. . . . (*A general chorus of hallo Margaret, good morning Prime Minister, as those sitting stand.*) I do hope everyone got some sleep after last night. Willy, dear, I think you were a *hero*! Come along in everyone. . . . (*A uniformed attendant has opened the doors to the Cabinet Room itself, and they start to troop through chatting.*) The press have been so silly about it this morning. . . .

7. INT. THE CABINET ROOM. DAY

A full Cabinet in progress. The brown baize cloth of the table is covered with papers, originally in their bright red cabinet folders. We track round the table taking in ministers (at Dec. 1980) their papers, the room itself, the silent secretariat in attendance.

CARRINGTON (*voice*): . . . The instability of the regime is at the heart of it. The military junta have utterly failed to control the economy or inflation, which roars away like a volcano. . . . (*camera settles on* CARRINGTON). . . . It is a government of terror, torture and execution without trial, thousands of people a year, not unlike the Gestapo. They *could* make such a hotheaded gesture as to invade; personally I think it unlikely.

PYM: Prime Minister, the Ministry of Defence is in possession of the Argentine military plan to invade the islands – drawn up in 1976 and revised every year.

WHITELAW: Prime Minister, do we have a planned response to that?

PM (*to* PYM): Secretary of State?

PYM: We do, but it requires substantial notice of their intentions – at least a week.

CARRINGTON: Which they're hardly likely to give!

WHITELAW: Well, we can't keep half the army and navy down there, just in case!

PYM: We've got the ice-breaker HMS *Endurance* patrolling in the area, of course. She's a form of deterrent. And a nuclear-powered sub could always be despatched from Gibraltar.

CARRINGTON: How long would that take to arrive?

PYM: Seven to ten days, Prime Minister.

CARRINGTON: There is another factor, Prime Minister. The Minister of State acknowledges that his parliamentary reception over leaseback was a grave blow . . . (*Murmurs of disgraceful! It was a beargarden etc.*) But the new President of Argentina, President Viola, is about to be installed. This *could* herald a more realistic policy towards negotiation – less sabre-rattling.

PYM: My Ministry's assessment of Viola is that he is weak, and the military junta may well gain in power as a result.

WHITELAW: *More* sabre-rattling.

PYM: Yes.

WHITELAW: Hm.

JOHN NOTT: Perhaps, Prime Minister, we should wait and see how he turns out. Before deciding the next step.

Several ministers mutter agreement.

PM: Is that the general opinion? (*Murmur of concurrence. Some ministers nod or raise their pencils.*) Very well. But we must *not* loose sight of this one. Thank you everyone.

All rise, chattering, and start putting their folders away in their boxes.

WHITELAW (*cheerfully*): Argentina. Where the nuts come from.

CARRINGTON (*grinning*): No, no, that's Brazil!

WHITELAW: Is it? It's all Comic Opera Land, anyhow. Do you know, they haven't fought *any*one for over a hundred years, except each other?

CARRINGTON *laughs!*

8. ARGENTINE NEWSFILM

Blare of tin trumpets, clatter of hooves, and the presidential procession swings into view in the crowded streets of Buenos Aires. Weedy cavalry in bright Ruritanian uniforms ride alongside. It is indeed close to Comic Opera Land. The crowds cheer and throw streamers.

9. EXT. BALCONY OF THE CASA ROSADA, BUENOS AIRES (PRESIDENTIAL PALACE CUM GOVERNMENT HOUSE)

LIEUTENANT-GENERAL LEOPOLDO GALTIERI *swears in the new president,* LIEUTENANT-GENERAL VIOLA, *on the balcony. Both have their right hands raised.*

GALTIERI: . . . and will administer justice to the Argentine people, guarding their honour, protecting their lives, to the utmost of your ability?

VIOLA: So help me God.

A military band strikes up the Argentine national anthem, and the crowd applauds, as GALTIERI *invests* VIOLA *with the presidential baton and sash, saluting him and shaking hands.* VIOLA *steps forward and waves to the crowd, which breaks into rhythmical chanting: 'Ar-gen-tin-a! Ar-gen-tin-a!'.* THE MILITARY JUNTA *stands back in a little semicircle around him, clapping politely:-*

(1) GALTIERI, *head of the army. A big, handsome, hard-drinking cavalry officer with hearty, drill-ground manner.*

(2) ANAYA, *head of the navy. Slim, vulpine and unsmiling, dressed in white admiral's uniform; a hard man whose voice betrays no flicker of warmth or humanity.*

(3) DOZO, *head of the air force. A crumpled teddy bear of a man, the most intelligent and liberal of the three.)*

10. INT. GALTIERI'S PRIVATE APARTMENT, BUENOS AIRES

Close shot of a television set. The new President addresses us on screen, with enthusiasm.

VIOLA: . . . Freedom of the press, responsibility exercised, is essential to democracy. In future, *all* Government decisions will be made known to the press. (*Track back.* GALTIERI *and* ANAYA *stand watching.* GALTIERI *has a large tumbler of whisky, and chain-smokes.*) The Government will listen to criticism, however harsh it may be.

ANAYA (*dead pan*): Of course we will.

VIOLA: Our new friends in the United States of America continue to be generous in their support and advice to the Argentine people. (GALTIERI *growls in annoyance at this.*) So with the help of Jesus, *and* President Reagan, a new and happier page in the noble history of our country is about to be written. God Bless Argentina.

Blare of national anthem. GALTIERI *switches it off. The luxury apartment is on the twenty-second floor of the Avenue Sucre, in the most fashionable suburb of Buenos Aires. A large balcony overlooks the park. There are a great many American gadgets of one sort or another, and much evidence of whisky and cigarette consumption – all part of the macho image.*

GALTIERI (*annoyed*): He shouldn't have said that.

ANAYA: About the US?

GALTIERI: There's no need to rub our noses in it. (*He pours himself more whisky.*) We can stand on our own two feet.

ANAYA: The US have been whining at us for years about human rights. Now they need us.

GALTIERI (*angry*): Do you want American bases here, Americans on our ships to tell you what to do? We don't want them down here starting the Third World War!

ANAYA: The First World War was a conflict of armies; the second, of nations; the third will be a conflict of ideologies. *That*'s not going to happen in Buenos Aires.

GALTIERI *ponders this, grunts, offers packet*

GALTIERI: Have some popcorn.

ANAYA (*screwing up face*): How can you eat that filth!

GALTIERI: What's wrong with it? You ought to try some.

He crams it into his mouth, washing it down with Glenfiddich. ANAYA *stares out of the windows at the tree-tops.*

ANAYA: I give him six months.

GALTIERI: Who?

ANAYA: Viola.

GALTIERI: But we only just invested him!

ANAYA: – so do the Americans. (*turning to Galtieri*) Then we have a new President.

GALTIERI (*waving the idea away*): No, no. I'd be no good.

ANAYA: You would be very good . . . provided you came to an agreement with the Navy.

GALTIERI (*suspicious*): Agreement, what agreement?

ANAYA (*lightly*): Certain matters could be planned between

us – the future of the navy, certain *territorial* matters . . . you are the natural candidate. (GALTIERI *thinks about it, clearly not for the first time.* ANAYA *watches him.*) Are you still going to that dinner at the US Embassy tonight?

GALTIERI: Yes?

ANAYA: They think so too.

11. INT. US EMBASSY, BUENOS AIRES

A small dinner party to celebrate the installation of President Viola. GALTIERI, *in mess-jacket with decorations, is flanked by* TOM ENDERS, *the Assistant Secretary of State for Latin-American Affairs in the State Department, and* JEAN KIRKPATRICK, *the US Ambassador to the United Nations. ('Too-Tall Enders' is 6 foot 8 inches tall, an extremely clever and respected, laconic, foreign service and intelligence officer;* KIRKPATRICK, *fifty-six, is rasping and abrasive; she is sometimes known as Reagan's battleaxe.)*

The Ambassador, HARRY SCHLAUDEMANN, *is on his feet.*

SCHLAUDEMANN: . . . and we are most heartened that the new President should have at his elbow one of the most respected figures in Southern America – Argentina's General Patton – Leopoldo Galtieri. (*applause.*) The General clearly sees the advantage to the whole world of the closest co-operation between the forces of Argentina and the United States, towards the creation of a South Atlantic Treaty Organization – SATO – to match NATO. Such an organization would further reduce any possibility of a Third World War.

GALTIERI: (*impressively*): The First World War was a conflict of armies; the second was of nations; the third will be of ideologies. *That*'s not going to happen in Buenos Aires.

Murmurs of admiration at this soldierly wisdom.

SCHLAUDEMANN: I had the great honour of accompanying the General on his recent visit to the USA. It was one of the hallmarks of his sturdy independence of mind that he chose as the main event of his visit an all-day tour of Disneyland – such is his earnest desire to plumb the deep wells of American character. (*patter of applause.*) So that when, earlier today, we raised our glasses to the new President, we raised them also to the men at his elbow, and we thought not only of the present, but of the future.

He sits. Applause, then general chatter. JEAN KIRKPATRICK *turns to* GALTIERI *with a warm smile.*

KIRKPATRICK: You've no idea what a pleasure it is to be able to say those things openly again!

GALTIERI (*courteous little bow*): That goes for us too, Mrs Kirkpatrick.

ENDERS: I don't know that our sanctions ever really worked, did they General?

GALTIERI: We missed the visits of our American brother officers.

KIRKPATRICK: Well, that was mutual! (ENDERS *murmurs agreement.*) Viola's wrong to start severing his links with the army. (*confidentially*) Any future President must be sure to retain his military position.

ENDERS (*hurriedly*): As usual, Mrs Kirkpatrick is voicing a personal opinion!

KIRKPATRICK: Oh come on, Tom – it's common sense! – and the first thing Viola will learn!

12. INT. THE PRESIDENT'S STUDY CASA ROSADA, BUENOS AIRES. NIGHT

VIOLA *sits behind his marble-topped desk, anxiously watching* ANAYA *finish reading a twenty-page document.* ANAYA *places it carefully back on the desk.*

ANAYA (*eventually*): It is too soon for such national reforms. The navy would not support them.

VIOLA: Perhaps we should *ask* the navy?

ANAYA (*looking him straight in the eyes*): You just have.

13. INT. THE FOREIGN SECRETARY'S ROOM, FOREIGN OFFICE

A major Foreign Office meeting, chaired by RIDLEY. *Those present around the long table include* ANTHONY WILLIAMS, *the British Ambassador in Buenos Aires (who has flown back specially);* ROBIN FEARN; *and seven others –*

RIDLEY: You've all got this, I suppose. (*he holds up a copy of a letter.*) The islanders want a total freeze on *all* negotiations with Argentina!

Anger and exasperation all round.

WILLIAMS: I have to say that in my view this greatly increases the chances of the Argentines taking direct military action.

RIDLEY: Robin?

FEARN: You all have the Joint Intelligence Committee's assessment of the likely Argentine reaction. (*All open and study the blue files.*) As you see, they plan eight graduated steps of increasing pressure on us; starting with a return to the UN to denounce us for bad faith; building to an air and fuel blockade and embargo to the islands; up to stage five – an invasion of South Georgia; right up to stage eight, a full-scale invasion of the islands themselves.

WILLIAMS: Which we couldn't possibly resist. I think this underlines why I insisted on this meeting – we must have a policy!

They all stare at the file gloomily.

FEARN: The only way to prevent this is to persuade the islanders to change their minds.

RIDLEY: Too much persuasion, and you create a political

earthquake; too little – and the Argentines get trigger happy. Right?

He looks around the table; no one demurs.

14. INT. THE FOREIGN SECRETARY'S ROOM, HOUSE OF COMMONS

RIDLEY *and* CARRINGTON, *angry and irritable on both sides.*

CARRINGTON: Not even the *gentlest* pressure! I forbid it!

RIDLEY: Then they will never change their minds!

CARRINGTON: Well that is their privilege!

RIDLEY: Then you're prepared to risk Argentina's reaction?

CARRINGTON (*exasperated*): Nicholas, we've no option! I don't *like* it, any more than you do!

Pause.

RIDLEY: How long do you think we've got?

CARRINGTON: Before this starts? (*He stabs his finger on the distinctive blue JIC file. Ridley nods.*) The first stage or two should give us reasonable warning.

RIDLEY: Provided no one winks to the Argentines that they should just go ahead.

CARRINGTON (*throwing file down*): Ridiculous.

RIDLEY: Is it? (*turning to him accusingly*) What about the withdrawal of HMS *Endurance*?

CARRINGTON (*angrily*): That's been on the cards for years!

RIDLEY: The *one* ship we have protecting the Falklands, the one ship to be withdrawn!

CARRINGTON (*shouting at him*): Well, we just can't afford to keep it there! *Whatever* happens in Buenos Aires!

15. EXT. BALCONY OF THE CASA ROSADA, BUENOS AIRES

The installation of GALTIERI *as President.* THE CHIEF JUSTICE *invests him with the presidential sash and baton, as military bands play and crowds cheer.* ANAYA *and* DOZO *clap politely.*

16. INT. THE PRESIDENT'S STUDY, CASA ROSADA

A ring of chairs face the massive presidential desk. In them sit: ADMIRAL ANAYA; AIR-MARSHAL DOZO; *the new Foreign Minister,* DR COSTA-MENDEZ *(a cripple from childhood, he hobbles about on two sticks, which does not apparently harm his reputation as a short and cheerful lady-killer);* ENRIQUE ROS *his deputy – slim, smooth and debonair;* DR ROBERTO ALEMANN, *the new Economy Minister, a grim disciple of Professor Milton Friedman. He reads from notes.* GALTIERI *moves between his desk and the window, smoking a Churchillian cigar, still wearing his sash.*

ALEMANN: The economic package I shall present to Cabinet is very severe: we float the exchange rate, freeze public sector spending totally, increase taxation by 90 per cent, and cut defence spending by half.

ANAYA (*smoothly*): Except for the navy.

ALEMANN (*turning to him*): *All* armed forces.

ANAYA (*not turning a hair*): Except for the navy.

DOZO (*appalled*): It's suicidal! We'd be back to rioting, martial law, an ungovernable country!

ANAYA: You cannot tiptoe when you have inflation of 150 per cent.

GALTIERI (*grunt*): The army will deal with unrest.

ALEMANN: I must know I have the junta's support for this.

ANAYA: You have it. Except . . . (*he waves a forefinger in the direction of Alemann's list*) . . . that little mistake. Next?

(ROS *and* DOZO *are visibly appalled.*)

GALTIERI: Foreign Minister?

COSTA-MENDEZ (*reading from notes*): One: increased *rapprochement* with the USA. Two: active participation in the anti-communist drive in Nicaragua and El Salvador. Three: a more aggressive policy towards our neighbour Chile.

ANAYA: Four: a plan to recover the Malvinas by the end of the year.

ROS (*startled*): But I am just about to negotiate this – by diplomacy.

ANAYA (*expressionless*): This will strengthen your hand.

ALEMANN: You mean, it is a bluff?

ANAYA: Of course it is bluff. (*He suddenly smiles at* ALEMANN.) I said a *plan*, that would be leaked; not action.

GALTIERI (*to the meeting*): The one thing that every Argentine dreams of, the one thing that would unite our country while these hard but necessary things (*indicating Alemann's list*) go through!

A pause, while ROS, COSTA-MENDEZ *and* ALEMANN *digest this.*

ALEMANN: But bluff.

ANAYA (*nodding*): Bluff.

ROS: A telegram of warning then, to Lord Carrington.

ANAYA: Copy to Washington.

COSTA-MENDEZ: To General Haig?

GALTIERI: No. (*thoughtfully.*) Mrs Kirkpatrick.

17. INT. THE ANTE-ROOM (TYPISTS AND SECRETARIAT) TO THE SECRETARY OF STATE'S ROOM, STATE DEPARTMENT, WASHINGTON

JEAN KIRKPATRICK, *clutching signal, is arguing noisily with* TOM ENDERS.

KIRKPATRICK: But I know he's in there!

ENDERS: That's not the point.

KIRKPATRICK: Al Haig is through that door and I have to see him.

ENDERS: If it's a diplomatic telegram he'll have his own copy!

KIRKPATRICK: Not of this one he won't!

HAIG *has appeared in his doorway, glowering angrily. He is fifty-eight and glows with vigour, like a health advertisement.*

HAIG: Not of what one?

KIRKPATRICK (*holding it up*): Top secret, from Costa-Mendez, in Buenos Aires.

HAIG: So your solution is to de-secretize it, decibelwise?

He gestures her in.

18. INT. THE SECRETARY OF STATE'S ROOM, STATE DEPARTMENT

As AL HAIG *reads the signal –*

KIRKPATRICK (*pointing*): It says time for negotiation is running out. It says the US should take sides.

HAIG: But why copy this to you?

KIRKPATRICK: Perhaps the Argentines know who their friends are.

HAIG (*stung*): Oh really? And do they also know who the hell decides foreign policy in Washington?

KIRKPATRICK: I know all about Latin-American policy, Mr Secretary; *I've* spent years at it.

This second dig strikes home as well.

HAIG (*angry*): Well, you tell the British – Ridley, Nicholas Ridley . . .

KIRKPATRICK: There's been a change. Richard Luce.

HAIG: You tell who*ever* the hell it is the United States will not get involved in some crazy spat over a bunch of ice-cold rocks on the edge of the world. They can fight this one out themselves!

19. INT. ANAYA'S STUDY, ADMIRALTY HOUSE, BUENOS AIRES. NIGHT

ANAYA *working alone in a pool of light from his desk lamp. It is 10 pm; traffic can be heard outside.*

ANAYA (*voice over*): Appreciation of the point of view of Mrs Margaret Thatcher in the event of the liberation of the Malvinas by the armed forces of Argentina. (*He produces school ruler and underlines it.*) One. Position of warships and nuclear-powered submarines of British Royal Navy, also of HMS *Endurance*. (*He consults typed intelligence reports in neat stacks and files on his desk.*) One, A. Ships engaged in Fleet exercise 'Springtrain' off Gibraltar and Casablanca. Type 42 destroyers: *Coventry*, *Glasgow*, *Sheffield* . . .

MIX (TIME LAPSE)

ANAYA *is walking the room, thinking it through. It is 2 am. The streets outside are quiet now.*

ANAYA (*voice over*): . . . use of the veto in Security Council. Britain will obtain five or six votes. The non-aligned states will vote on an anti-colonial basis.

ANAYA (*suddenly aloud*): The Russians will veto, on the same basis!

ANAYA (*voice over*): Therefore, no mandatory vote in the Security Council. (*He returns to his desk quickly, and continues to write.*) The EEC in Brussels will vote for sanctions against Argentina on the use of force, but abandon them on the failure of Security Council vote. The Organization of American States and the signatories to the Treaty of Rio will . . .

MIX (TIME LAPSE)

First dawn light creeps through the windows. One or two birds have begun the dawn chorus.

ANAYA (*voice over*): . . . pressure on the domestic political grasp of Margaret Thatcher, which is fully stretched. (*He ticks off a typed list.*) Two million unemployed; two hundred company bankruptcies each week; Northern Ireland; foreign investment moving overseas.

ANAYA (*aloud*): Therefore . . . she lacks the political *will* to make military response.

ANAYA (*voice over*): Conclusion. In the event of the forces of Argentina liberating the Malvinas . . . (*He taps the separate sheets of paper, spread over the table*). No armed response from the UK; no effective response from the USA; no economic sanctions for longer than one week; no mandatory vote in the United Nations. Therefore, Argentina can recover the Malvinas at – practically – no – cost.

He stares at this conclusion for a moment, as if barely able to believe it.

20. INT. THE PRESIDENT'S STUDY, CASA ROSADA, BUENOS AIRES. NIGHT

The junta in session. DOZO *is reading the appreciation.* ANAYA *is unusually animated.*

ANAYA: . . . of course, we will continue very hard to reach a diplomatic solution. The world will see we are the long-injured party, finally driven to such desperation . . . (*He waves towards the appreciation.*) As we agreed.

GALTIERI *nods.* DOZO *looks up.*

DOZO: "Agreed"?

GALTIERI: There has been some discussion between us.

DOZO *looks between them, then lays the document on the desk.*

DOZO: Timing?

GALTIERI: HMS *Endurance* will be withdrawn in October.

ANAYA: Which will leave a total defence force on the island of forty-two Royal Marines.

DOZO: And the nearest British base is. . . . ?

ANAYA: Belize. Five thousand miles away.

All three are conscious of the eeriness of the situation – almost as if they were being invited to invade.

DOZO (*shrug*): The air force has little role in this.

ANAYA (*smoothly*): It is a naval operation.

GALTIERI: October, then. In eight months. (*He looks questioningly at* ANAYA, *who shrugs; they both look at* DOZO; *Dozo nods.*) Unless Divine Providence intervenes.

21. EXT. NIGHT SKY

Ablaze with stars. Sound of radio signals, morse code etc.

REX HUNT (*voice over*): "Governor Falkland Islands to Foreign and Commonwealth Office, London. Attention Mr

Luce. Urgent and secret. (*Tilting slowly down to show the aerials and saucer-receivers of the Foreign Office receiving station at Hanslope Park.*) I have this morning received a signal from the island of South Georgia. Argentine naval vessel *Bahia Buen Suceso* has been observed at deserted Leith Harbour. . . . ."

22. INT. FOREIGN OFFICE, CYPHER AND TELEGRAM DUTY OFFICE

Close shot of the telegram as it emerges jerkily from the machine, like a telex.

HUNT (*voice over*): "A party of civilians have established themselves ashore, claiming to be scrap-metal merchants. Shots have been fired, notices defaced and the Argentine flag raised. . . . ."

23. INT. FOREIGN OFFICE CORRIDORS/LUCE'S OFFICE

Close shot of a file of signals and FCO telegrams under the arm of A MESSENGER, *as he walks along corridor.*

HUNT (*voice over*): "Orders to leave, or to register with the proper authorities, have been ignored. (MESSENGER *enters Luce's room and places the telegrams on the Minister of State's desk.* LUCE *starts to flick through them.*) This is the second such violation in four months. (LUCE *stops at this telegram, and starts to read it.*) I have consulted Captain Barker of HMS *Endurance*, at present here in Falkland Sound, and request he be ordered to sail to South Georgia with all despatch to *enforce* eviction. . . . ."

LUCE *rises, telegram in hand.*

24. INT. THE FOREIGN SECRETARY'S ROOM, FOREIGN OFFICE

CARRINGTON *is reading the telegram,* LUCE *at his shoulder.*

HUNT (*voice over*): "In my view, the Argentine Navy may be using these men as a front to establish an Argentine presence on South Georgia."

CARRINGTON: The Falklands to South Georgia is . . . ?

LUCE: Eight hundred miles.

CARRINGTON: Tell our Ambassador to make the strongest protest. But we mustn't over-react; an over-reaction is perhaps what they want.

He stares at the telegram thoughtfully.

LUCE: I'll have to say something in the House.

CARRINGTON (*looking up sharply*): Play it down. Don't be provoked.

25. INT. HOUSE OF COMMONS

RICHARD LUCE *is at the despatch box. He is doing his best to make light of what he says.*

LUCE: . . . most of the men left, following diplomatic representations to Buenos Aires. A small number, however, remains, with their equipment. Her Majesty's Government is, er, 'making arrangements to assist their departure'.

He sits. Some chuckling round the House, and buzz of amused chatter about 'scrap-metal merchants'. DENIS HEALEY, *however, is not amused. Almost incredulous, he lumbers to his feet, huge eyebrows raised.*

SPEAKER: Mr Denis Healey.

HEALEY: Is it not the case that the Argentine party planted an Argentine *flag* on this British territory?

LUCE (*earnestly wanting to cool it*): For a short time, the Argentine flag was planted. It has now been removed.

He sits. HEALEY *rises a second time.*

HEALEY: Could this incident be connected with the Argentine threat to take *unilateral* action, unless negotiations really progressed?

26. INT. THE FOREIGN MINISTER'S ROOM, FOREIGN MINISTRY, BUENOS AIRES

COSTA-MENDEZ *is dressed formally. He is checking a typed sheet.* ROS *enters.*

ROS: He's here.

COSTA-MENDEZ: Wait. (*He signs the paper.*) Right.

ROS *goes out.* COSTA-MENDEZ *rises, hobbles to the middle of the room, and adopts an expression of heated indignation. The British Ambassador,* ANTHONY WILLIAMS, *enters. He leans on one stick.*

WILLIAMS: Good morning, Foreign Minister.

COSTA-MENDEZ: Good morning. (*A perfunctory handshake.* COSTA-MENDEZ *then reads from a typed page.*) 'The Ministry of Foreign Affairs expresses the deepest concern to Her Britannic Majesty's Government for an insult and outrage perpetrated at the Offices of the Argentine Air Force on the Malvinas Islands.'

WILLIAMS (*dry*): Oh really?

COSTA-MENDEZ: 'On the night of 21 March, the offices were forcibly entered, a British Union Jack hung over the Argentine flag, and the words "Tit for tat you buggers" written across the desk with toothpaste.'

WILLIAMS: With what?

COSTA-MENDEZ: 'The Argentine Government views this deliberate insult as most harmful to their peaceful endeavours to obtain a negotiated settlement of the Malvinas problem.'

COSTA-MENDEZ *thrusts the paper at* WILLIAMS, *and stumps back behind his desk.*

WILLIAMS (*looking up from the communiqué*): What sort of toothpaste?

COSTA-MENDEZ: I've no idea.

WILLIAMS: *Argentinian* toothpaste, or –

COSTA-MENDEZ: I must insist that, to defuse this regrettable situation, HMS *Endurance* is instructed immediately to turn around, and steam away from Malvinas waters!

WILLIAMS (*with communiqué*): Actually there are two G's in 'buggers'.

27. INT. PRESIDENT'S STUDY, THE CASA ROSADA/ANAYA'S STUDY ADMIRALTY HOUSE, BUENOS AIRES

Close shots of GALTIERI *and* ANAYA, *on the telephone to each other.*

GALTIERI (*heavily*): I'm not having innocent Argentine citizens seized by Royal Marines, frog-marched up a British gangplank –

ANAYA (*interrupting*): Leopoldo –

GALTIERI: – and thrown out of South Georgia with the whole world watching! That island belongs to us!

ANAYA: I can send a brigade of marines, to protect them.

GALTIERI: And what happens if the British get there first?

ANAYA (*calmly*): I will intercept them. By force.

GALTIERI (*taken aback*): On the high seas?

28. INT. THE FOREIGN SECRETARY'S ROOM, FOREIGN OFFICE.

Midnight. CARRINGTON *is drafting a telegram in a pool of desk light. A* SECRETARY *stands at his elbow, as he scribbles.*

CARRINGTON (*voice over*): . . . and make it crystal clear that we urge Mr Haig personally to intervene with the Argentine Government.

Telephone buzzes, THE SECRETARY *picks it up.*

SECRETARY: Yes? Yes, Prime Minister.

He hands the receiver to CARRINGTON, *as his boss hands him the draft.*

CARRINGTON: Yes, Margaret.

29. INT. THE PRIME MINISTER'S STUDY, 10 DOWNING STREET

MRS THATCHER *working in a pool of light from her desk lamp,* JOHN NOTT *at her elbow. Her desk is stacked with papers on other matters; now she holds a 'raw' intelligence report from GCHQ, Cheltenham.*

PM: Two Argentine corvettes have broken away from the Uruguayan manoeuvres and are steaming towards South Georgia.

30. INT. THE FOREIGN SECRETARY'S ROOM, FOREIGN OFFICE

CARRINGTON *grimaces.*

CARRINGTON: We've been trying not to worry you about South Georgia. Where's the Chief of Defence Staff?

31. INT. THE PRIME MINISTER'S STUDY, 10 DOWNING STREET

PM (*to Nott*): Where's Admiral Lewin?

NOTT *leans forward to speak to the receiver.*

NOTT: In New Zealand.

PM: Can we review this on the plane to Brussels in the morning?

NOTT (*to receiver*): Those corvettes – they're armed with Exocets.

32. INT. THE FOREIGN SECRETARY'S ROOM, FOREIGN OFFICE

CARRINGTON: I'm just telling Nicko Henderson to tell the Americans they've just got to stop this!

33. INT. THE SECRETARY OF STATE'S ROOM, STATE DEPARTMENT

AL HAIG *stands beaming a welcome, as an aide opens the door.*

AIDE (*announcing*): Sir Nicholas Henderson.

HAIG: Nicko!

HENDERSON *comes steaming in, letter in hand. Normally urbane and studiously rumpled of both dress and hair, now he is angry.*

HENDERSON: What do you mean, 'even-handed approach'?

HAIG (*cheerfully*): The Argentines are good friends of ours now, you know that! You're *both* good friends!

HENDERSON (*incredulously*): Are you seriously putting Her Majesty's Government on the same footing as a bunch of fifth-rate, comic-opera thugs, who –

HAIG: They won't fight! It's bluff!

34. INT. THE FOREIGN SECRETARY'S ROOM, FOREIGN OFFICE

CARRINGTON *stands behind his desk, blasting the unfortunate American Chargé d'Affaires,* ED STREATOR.

CARRINGTON: *Aggression* is about to be perpetrated in the South Atlantic! Whose side are you on?

STREATOR: Surely to mediate between two friends is –

CARRINGTON: We don't want mediation! (*thumps desk*) We want a condemnation of the use of force! – in the face of the whole world!

STREATOR (*wide-eyed*): One – little – rocky – barren – ice-bound – island?

35. INT. ANAYA'S STUDY, ADMIRALTY HOUSE/THE FOREIGN MINISTER'S ROOM, FOREIGN MINISTRY, BUENOS AIRES

Cross-cutting ANAYA *and* COSTA-MENDEZ *on the telephone to each other.* ANAYA *is pushing hard.*

ANAYA: . . . and so we have the perfect *casus belli* for immediate repossession of the Malvinas!

Pause.

COSTA-MENDEZ (*faintly*): What did you say?

ANAYA: The British behaviour is intolerable! They deploy those marines, that old ice-breaker. . . . .

36. INT. THE PRESIDENT'S STUDY, CASA ROSADA, BUENOS AIRES

GALTIERI, ANAYA *and* DOZO, *all on their feet.* GALTIERI *walks about, angry at being manipulated.*

DOZO: It is the *lack* of British response that amazes me! They make a great noise, but –

GALTIERI (*to Anaya*): We reoccupy the Malvinas to *prevent* the British using it to extend their piracy?

ANAYA: Exactly. (*spreads his hands.*) *Fait accompli.*

DOZO: But we had agreed a date! October!

ANAYA: Which we can bring forward! . . . .

37. INT. THE FOREIGN MINISTER'S ROOM, FOREIGN MINISTRY, BUENOS AIRES

COSTA-MENDEZ, ROS, ANAYA, GALTIERI.

COSTA-MENDEZ: But you cannot mount an operation like this overnight!

GALTIERI (*grunting*): The planners have been working on Operation Azul for some weeks.

ROS (*astonished*): Azul?

ANAYA: The Fleet is at sea on the Uruguayan exercise. We simply change their objective.

GALTIERI: We must *exploit* what is handed to us! – on a plate!

COSTA-MENDEZ *still can't work out exactly how he has been cheated.*

COSTA-MENDEZ: But . . . those scrap-metal merchants. . . ?

ANAYA: Perfectly bona fide. (*He suddenly shouts; we hear the sharp edge of fanaticism in his voice.*) Your job is not to obstruct us! Your job is to go to the United Nations and explain!

38. ON BOARD PLANE

The PM *and* CARRINGTON *sit side by side at a table covered with briefing papers and telegrams. They are en route to an EEC meeting in Brussels.*

PM: John Nott thinks we should send submarines now. To support *Endurance*.

CARRINGTON: I think we should.

PM: The nearest is at Gibraltar – up to ten days to get there.

CARRINGTON: The Argentines have built up a dangerous head of steam – it gives them very little room to manoeuvre.

PM: Anti-government riots are not the best platform for launching a war.

CARRINGTON: Riots? (*The* PM *finds and hands him the telegram, pointing to a section.*) There was a leader in *La Prensa* which said: 'The only thing that can save this Government now, is a war.'

The PM *looks up slowly, digesting this.*

39. ARGENTINE NEWSFILM

Anti-government demonstrations and ferocious mob violence in the streets of Buenos Aires. The military and police counter-attack is brutal in the extreme, and ends with shooting.

40. INT. JOHN NOTT'S OFFICE, MINISTRY OF DEFENCE

NOTT *getting his overcoat from the cupboard, as* A SECRETARY *and his private secretary,* JOHN WILKINSON, *gather papers into files and a despatch box. The direct buzzer goes.* THE SECRETARY *presses the switch of the loudspeaker phone.*

SECRETARY: Mr Nott's office.

LEACH (*distort*): May I come along? It is important.

NOTT (*leaning over*): I'm just on my way to the Commons. To hear Richard Luce.

LEACH (*distort*): That's why I want to see you.

NOTT: Right.

NOTT *switches off, puts on coat, takes papers etc.* ADMIRAL SIR HENRY LEACH *enters. He is sharp, erect, slim, precise, professional to his fingertips.*

LEACH: Good afternoon, Secretary of State.

NOTT (*continuing to prepare*): I am listening, Henry.

LEACH: I called a senior ops staff meeting this afternoon. We reviewed the options presented to us following the despatch of the submarines to the South Atlantic –

NOTT: Yes?

LEACH: If things should get worse. (*they start to go*) If the Argentines should invade the Falkland Islands, for instance.

NOTT: Yes.

41. INT. CORRIDOR, MINISTRY OF DEFENCE

NOTT *walks rapidly along,* LEACH *at his elbow,* a SECRETARY *following with box and papers.* WILKINSON follows.

LEACH (*continuing*): Argentina has a substantial navy – at least six ships fitted with Exocet, four submarines, a good carrier, an air force of two hundred planes fully capable of attacking any British Task Force approaching by sea.

NOTT: Yes.

LEACH: The difficulties of operating against such a force eight thousand miles from Fleet Headquarters, would be immense.

42. INT. LIFT, MINISTRY OF DEFENCE

LEACH, NOTT, WILKINSON and SECRETARY *going down.*

LEACH (*continuing*): Therefore we rejected any task force that did not embrace *all* forces – aircraft-carriers, submarines, escorts – a full amphibious assault force.

The lift stops and the doors open, but NOTT *does not move.*

NOTT (*staring at Leach*): What?

LEACH: If things *do* get worse, we have only two military options. One is to do nothing.

NOTT: And the other?

LEACH: To send in the Fleet.

NOTT: The *whole* Fleet?

LEACH: Substantially.

NOTT (*appalled*): Nothing in between?

LEACH: Nothing.

NOTT: I see. (NOTT *leaves the lift, dazed by this news, followed by* WILKINSON and the SECRETARY. LEACH *presses the button to reascend, but* NOTT *suddenly reappears.*) The *entire* Fleet?

LEACH: Yes. You see –

NOTT (*holds up hand*): I get the point.

43. INT. MINISTERIAL CAR

Going down Whitehall. NOTT *and* WILKINSON *side by side, still dazed by the announcement.*

WILKINSON (*wonderingly*): A full British battle fleet putting to sea in anger. Nothing like that's happened since Suez.

NOTT (*shuddering*): Can we leave Suez out of this conversation?

WILKINSON: Sorry.

NOTT: It's one of those little words that irk.

44. INT. HOUSE OF COMMONS

LUCE *at the despatch box, concluding his statement.*

LUCE: ... further escalation of the dispute is in no one's interest. The question of security in the Falklands is being reviewed, though the House will understand ... (*gently underlining it*) ... that I prefer to say nothing in public about the steps we are taking.

He sits, hoping to goodness that no one is going to push him further on that. HEALEY *rises.*

SPEAKER: Mr Denis Healey.

HEALEY: I think the Minister of State's feeble statement will lead many to conclude that Her Majesty's Government's conduct of this affair has been both foolish and spineless! (*Cheerful hear, hears! from the Labour benches at this good knockabout stuff.* HEALEY *grins.*) I can understand that he may wish to say nothing – because he has nothing to say! (*much opposition mirth.*) If he has, he could surely be a little less bashful about it.

He sits. Labour cries of answer! answer! and jeering.

45. NOTT'S BEDROOM. NIGHT

NOTT *lies awake, eyes open in the dark. Bedside phone shrills.*

NOTT (*taking it*): Nott.

VOICE (*distort*): Duty office, Defence Ministry, sir. There was an emergency meeting of the Cabinet Intelligence Group (W) at 2.30 this morning.

NOTT (*turning on light*): Yes.

VOICE (*distort*): To assess signals monitored by GCHQ Cheltenham at one o'clock.

NOTT (*looking at his watch*): What signals, where from?

VOICE (*distort*): They've called a Joint Intelligence Committee at 7.30 in the Cabinet Office. Er, from the South Atlantic, sir.

46. INT. THE MINISTER OF DEFENCE'S ROOM, HOUSE OF COMMONS

JOHN WILKINSON *places a black despatch box on the desk, which is covered with papers his Minister is working through.*

WILKINSON: It's a Sigint assessment, South Atlantic, I think. The Cabinet office sent it urgently.

NOTT *grunts, produces a small brass key on his watch-chain, and unlocks it.*

NOTT: No it isn't. It's JIC.

WILKINSON: What?

NOTT *extracts a small red-covered loose-leaf booklet of about ten pages, and a black-bound annex.*

NOTT: You're not supposed to see this. (*He no more than glances at the first two pages before he is visibly shaken.*) Where's the Prime Minister?

WILKINSON: In her room. Do you want me to –

NOTT *has grabbed the two folders and left the room.*

47. INT. THE MAIN CORRIDOR FOREIGN OFFICE

RICHARD LUCE *striding along, with similar red and black folders. He encounters* ROBIN FEARN.

LUCE: I was coming to get you. Where's Peter Carrington?

FEARN: Tel Aviv at this moment. Humphrey Atkins is deputizing.

LUCE: Tell Humphrey I've got a JIC assessment I'm taking straight over to Downing Street.

FEARN: For the Prime Minister?

LUCE: Yes.

FEARN: She's at her room in the House.

LUCE: There, then.

48. INT. THE PRIME MINISTER'S ROOM, HOUSE OF COMMONS

A lofty, L-shaped room, very quiet and comfortable, with high Pugin-Gothic windows overlooking Palace Yard. In the long arm of the 'L', a half-size cabinet table with ten chairs; in the short arm, a ring of armchairs round the fireplace. JOHN NOTT *and the* PM *both have copies of the red and black folders, and are reading them. Close shot of the* PM. *She is shattered by what she reads.*

NOTT: Have you seen number 13 in the annex? (*he indicates it.*) We knew last night they were redeploying those warships. But not for this!

PM (*with very quiet fury*): I was assured, *absolutely* and *categorically*, that this could not happen!

A knock at the door. The PM *doesn't move or speak.* NOTT *himself rises and opens the door to the detectives' and secretaries' outer office.* LUCE *and* FEARN *enter.*

LUCE/FEARN: Good afternoon, Prime Minister.

She waves them to the table in silence. They sit. She finally looks up.

PM (*quietly*): You've been briefed on this?

LUCE: I have. Not Robin.

The PM *gestures to* NOTT, *and re-immerses herself in the JIC assessment.*

NOTT: Just after midnight the Argentine Fleet broke away from the exercises with Uruguay, and began steaming south at top speed. Their only aircraft-carrier, the *Veinticinco de Mayo*, left Puerto Belgrano twenty minutes later, and is heading straight for the Falkland Islands. And this . . . (*he indicates telegram 13 in the black annex.*) . . . direct intercept of a signal to the submarine *Santa Fè*. Ordering her to surface and carry out an immediate survey of beach landing sites round Port Stanley.

PM (*still very quiet*): Get Peter Carrington back. And the Chief of Defence Staff. Where's Admiral Leach?

NOTT: In Portsmouth. An official visit. I've signalled him to return immediately.

PM: We must get on to Reagan. The Americans must stop this!

49. INT. THE SECRETARY OF STATE'S ROOM, STATE DEPARTMENT

An angry HENDERSON; *a laid-back and sceptical* ENDERS; *and* HAIG, *who is reading a copy of the assessment.*

HENDERSON (*insisting*): I tell you they are invading!

ENDERS (*smiling at him*): It's just not possible, Mr Ambassador.

HENDERSON: It's there, it's in the intelligence reports! You think we've made it up?

HAIG (*very quiet, to* ENDERS): Why was I not informed of this?

ENDERS: What? (*shaken*) I had a categorical assurance from Costa-Mendez that they would not invade!

HAIG: Well he's made a fool of you. Get on to our Ambassador in Buenos Aires. Tell him to go and see Galtieri *now*, *tonight*, and demand to know what the hell he's playing at!

HENDERSON: Could not President Reagan –

HAIG: I'll see the President myself.

50. INT. THE PRESIDENT'S STUDY CASA ROSADA, BUENOS AIRES

AMBASSADOR SCHLAUDEMANN *enters briskly, typed sheet in hand. He stops in his tracks on seeing* GALTIERI, *in full uniform, standing stiffly to attention in front of his desk.*

SCHLAUDEMANN: Good evening, sir. (GALTIERI *sways very slightly. He is drunk.*) I have a personal message for you, from General Haig. (*He reads out*) 'Should *any* Argentine military action occur in the South Atlantic, for whatever reason, overwhelming pressure would be brought to bear on the Reagan administration immediately to abandon its new-found and highly promising relationship with Argentina.' (*He hands the sheet to* GALTIERI, *who ignores it.*) Do you have any comment?

GALTIERI: No.

SCHLAUDEMANN: Do you deny that military action is –

GALTIERI: I have no comment. (SCHLAUDEMANN *places the typed sheet on the President's desk, and turns to leave.*) Tell General Haig . . . (*He sways.* SCHLAUDEMANN *stops and watches him.*) Tell General Haig that *if* we should ever take such action . . . *if* – then he should acquiesce! (*He lifts his forefinger to emphasize, with alcoholic cunning.*) In return, he would receive our fullest co-operation for the new United States policy in the Southern Hemisphere! (SCHLAUDEMANN *turns and leaves.* GALTIERI *shouts after him*) You tell him that!

51. EXT. WHITEHALL

ADMIRAL LEACH, *in full admiral's uniform, papers in hand, dashes along the pavement from the Ministry of Defence to the*

House of Commons, half-scamper, half-run, narrowly missing traffic. Tourists are entranced by this Gilbertian spectacle.

52. INT. THE PRIME MINISTER'S ROOM, HOUSE OF COMMONS

Four more officials have joined the meeting, and the table is nearly full. FEARN *is entering from the outer office.*

FEARN: President Reagan has twice tried to speak to him – General Galtieri has refused to take his calls.

PM: *Refused*?

FEARN: On both occasions he was apparently told to try again later.

Exclamations of incredulity round the table.

NOTT: It could still be bluff.

PM (*at* NOTT): With the entire Argentine Navy at sea? – moving into position where it could invade the Islands within forty-eight hours? How quickly could we mount a Task Force?

NOTT (*yelp*): It's far too late for that!

PM: Not too late as a diplomatic lever, John.

LUCE: If they really *are* invading, Prime Minister, surely we should avoid doing anything provocative that could –

PM (*finally blowing*): Avoid anything provocative? What do you think *they*'re doing?

LUCE: I mean –

PM: Snatching and grabbing by force what they have failed to gain by honest negotiation! Avoid doing anything provocative?! Let them get away with this, and we send a signal round the entire world to *all* aggressive, greedy states and dictators that they can just march in and grab and get away with whatever they want, because the democracies are too feeble to say No!

The telephone on the table had quietly buzzed during this, and NOTT, *who answered, puts his hand over the mouthpiece.*

NOTT: Admiral Leach is outside.

PM: Thank God! Ask him please to come in. (LEACH *appears, and opens his mouth to say good evening. The* PM *stops him in his tracks, with ringing tones.*) How soon could you mobilize a full Task Force for the South Atlantic?

LEACH: It would have to be a balanced fleet, Prime Minister – not just a small squadron.

PM: Yes?

LEACH (*brisk and firm*): A group of our ships is currently off Gibraltar, on exercise. They could regroup and sail within twenty-four hours. The core of the Fleet is the two carriers, *Hermes* and *Invincible*. They are at Plymouth.

PM: It is now Wednesday night . . .

LEACH (*decisively*): They could sail by the first tide on Monday morning.

PM (*delighted*): You're certain of that?

LEACH: Absolutely. If you made the decision to prepare this evening.

PM (*to* NOTT): Do we need Cabinet approval for that?

NOTT: No, I can authorize emergency preparation.

PM: Then do so. It will show them we mean business. (*sudden shout*) Which we do!

53. INT. THE SECRETARY-GENERAL'S PANELLED CONFERENCE ROOM, UN BUILDING, NEW YORK

The Secretary-General, PEREZ DE CUELLAR; *the British Ambassador to the United Nations,* SIR ANTHONY PARSONS; *and the Argentine representative,* ENRIQUE ROS.

DE CUELLAR (*with some heat*): But why, Mr Ros, does your President refuse to take Mr Reagan's calls?

ROS: I am sure that is not correct! (*shakes head*) Most unlike him.

DE CUELLAR: I would like you to convey to your Government my utmost concern that they refrain from the use of force!

ROS: With respect, sir, that is a matter for the Security Council.

PARSONS (*nursing his sherry*): Which has been summoned in emergency session.

ROS (*startled*): What? But you need ten votes for that, Sir Anthony!

PARSONS (*with charming smile*): That's right.

DE CUELLAR: It meets (*glances at clock*) in three hours.

ROS *is startled.*

54. INT. ANTE-ROOM AND CORRIDOR OUTSIDE THE OVAL ROOM, THE WHITE HOUSE, WASHINGTON

HAIG *and* ENDERS *are hovering impatiently, waiting to go in.* PRESIDENT REAGAN'S PA *and personal telephonist is at her desk in this annex.*

HAIG (*impatiently*): Come on, come on . . .

THE PA *suddenly calls out excitedly, hand over the mouthpiece.*

PA: Sir! Mr Secretary! It's General Galtieri!

HAIG (*startled*): What? Put him straight through to the President!

PA: I can't! You know how he hates to be interrupted.

HAIG: Holy Moses. (*He starts to run to the oval room, with* ENDERS.) We're only trying to stop a war, lady. And we've got this skeleton in the cupboard called Suez.

ENDERS (*puffing*): That's not an American skeleton, it's a British one.

HAIG: You try telling that to the British.

55. INT. THE OVAL ROOM, THE WHITE HOUSE, WASHINGTON

REAGAN *is on the telephone, as* HAIG *and* ENDERS *enter hurriedly.*

REAGAN: Ycs, wcll of coursc I scc that, but – (*hand over mouthpiece*) What is it, who said you could come in?

HAIG (*panting*): It's Galtieri. On the line, waiting.

REAGAN (*to telephone*): I'm very sorry, but I'll have to ring you back. Very sorry, sir. (*He clicks off, and re-engages.*) Jean? Put him through.

GALTIERI (*distort*): I am through.

REAGAN (*urgently*): I am very glad and grateful to have a chance to talk to you at last, General. (*He gestures to* HAIG *to pick up the extension, which he does.*) We are getting more and more reports that you are about to invade those little islands down there, you know the ones I mean . . .

GALTIERI (*distort*): The Mal –

REAGAN: Never mind what we call them! Now listen –

56. INT. THE PRESIDENT'S STUDY, CASA ROSADA, BUENOS AIRES

GALTIERI *is at his desk, full ashtray in front of him, whisky at elbow.*

GALTIERI: The British have refused to acknowledge our sovereignty for a hundred and fifty years! Mr President, time has run out!

Pull back to show ANAYA, *listening on the extension earpiece.*

REAGAN (*distort*): Run out? But you can't start a war! *You* would be the aggressor, you must see that!

57. INT. THE OVAL ROOM, THE WHITE HOUSE, WASHINGTON

REAGAN (*earnestly*): Now look, I'll tell you what I'm going to do. I'll send you Vice-President George Bush to mediate – he can come first thing tomorrow morning, you understand?

GALTIERI (*distort*): There is no point in sending Mr Bush, it is too late!

REAGAN: Then will you assure me you are *not* invading? Hallo? Hallo?

HAIG (*on extension*): The line's gone dead.

REAGAN: He hung up on me! (*He bangs down the receiver angrily.*) He hung up!

58. ARGENTINE NEWSFILM

The Argentine fleet looms hugely through the darkness, at top speed.

59. INT. THE PRIME MINISTER'S STUDY, 10 DOWNING STREET

The PM *has been breakfasting on grapefruit juice and coffee, while preparing for the Cabinet. She looks drained and sleepless.*

PM: What do you mean, we *don't know*?

CARRINGTON: All lines to Port Stanley are dead. We simply don't know whether there's been an invasion or not.

PM (*rising, preparing to leave*): What about local Falkland Island radio? Don't we monitor that?

CARRINGTON: Apparently not

PM (*with gathering rage*): So I'm calling a Cabinet to discuss an invasion that we don't even know has happened!?

60. INT. THE MAIN STAIRCASE, 10 DOWNING STREET

The PM *and* CARRINGTON *descend.*

PM: Can't the Americans tell us anything?

CARRINGTON: They're waiting for news from *us*. The Foreign Office is obtaining a list of radio hams on the island, and trying to contact them.

PM (*with withering scorn*): Foreign Office! Useless when they're needed.

CARRINGTON: I don't think you can really –

PM: It's exactly what Norman's always said: an island is a piece of land entirely surrounded by advice from the Foreign Office. Until there's trouble.

61. INT. THE CABINET ROOM

The Cabinet in session. There is an air of paralysed shock.

PM: It could still be bluff. We must not over-react, but review our position in readiness for firm news. Foreign Secretary?

CARRINGTON (*with a shrug*): I can't take any further steps until I know the military position.

PM: Minister of Defence?

NOTT (*wretched*): The same.

CARRINGTON: Prime Minister, Richard Luce can't avoid

making a statement when the House assembles in an hour – what shall he say?

PM: As little as possible. I suppose the House may have to be recalled for an emergency debate on Saturday.

WHITELAW: *That* hasn't happened since the Suez Cr–

He hastily stops himself, and takes a drink of water.

PM (*burst of anger*): It's unbelievable that the Foreign Office can't tell us whether there's been an invasion or not!

TEBBIT: Are the lines to mainland Argentina dead as well?

CARRINGTON: No, apparently, they're functioning normally.

TEBBIT (*laconically*): Then perhaps we should ring up General Galtieri and ask *him* what's going on.

62. ARGENTINE NEWSFILM

An immense sea of 100,000 people packed into the Plaza Mayo in triumphal ecstacy – cheering themselves hoarse, waving flags, throwing flowers towards the balcony of the Casa Rosada.

63. EXT. BALCONY OF THE CASA ROSADA

THE JUNTA *acknowledging the crowd, delighted.* GALTIERI *steps forward, weeping with emotion, and raises his hands for silence.*

GALTIERI (*rhetorically*): The three Commanders-in-Chief have only interpreted the will of the Argentine people! It has been suppressed for a hundred and fifty years – but it is now visible in our streets!

64. ARGENTINE NEWSFILM

The immense crowd roars like the sea, and breaks into the chant 'Se siente, se siente, Galtieri Presidente!'

65. INT. HOUSE OF COMMONS

RICHARD LUCE *at the despatch box.*

LUCE: Even at this late stage, we earnestly hope the Argentine Government will reconsider their rejection of diplomatic channels to settle this dispute. (*forcefully*) The Falkland Islands are British, inhabited by British citizens who wish to remain British!

He sits to a rumble of agreement.

SPEAKER: Mr John Browne.

BROWNE (*drily*): Will my Right Honourable friend accept that, in a case like this, possession is likely to be about nine-tenths of the law?

66. AN ARGENTINE TELEVISION SCREEN

GALTIERI *addresses us directly, a Presidential Statement.*

GALTIERI: The recovery of the Malvinas will not mean the life of the islanders will be disrupted. On the contrary, everything will go on exactly as before. (*He looks us squarely in the eye.*) The British *forced* us to send an entire defensive force, including submarines, most of the air force, three battalions of commandos, four battalions of infantry, heavy artillery and tanks. (*He leans forward to emphasize.*) However, our intentions are *entirely peaceful.*

67. INT. THE FOREIGN SECRETARY'S ROOM, FOREIGN OFFICE

CARRINGTON *and* LUCE *who is distressed.*

CARRINGTON (*angrily*): There is no question of your resignation!

LUCE: It was my job to foresee this.

CARRINGTON: Do you think, as Foreign Secretary, that I'm any the less responsible?

LUCE: You can't be resp–

CARRINGTON (*fiercely*): Now listen. You can earn your salvation. I'm putting you in charge of co-ordinating the diplomatic offensive to get the Argies out. If they are in.

LUCE: The key to that is whether the Americans will help.

CARRINGTON: Well, get on the telephone and ask them!

68. INT. THE OVAL ROOM, THE WHITE HOUSE, WASHINGTON

The National Security Council in informal session, in the ring of armchairs at the fireplace end of the room. Those present are THE PRESIDENT, HAIG, ENDERS, JEAN KIRKPATRICK *and two others.*

HAIG: He demanded that Washington openly condemns Argentine military aggression; ambassadorial evacuation; and an embargo on all arms shipments to Buenos Aires.

REAGAN (*grunt*): Siding with the British.

HAIG: Exactly.

KIRKPATRICK (*angrily*): Which would buy us a hundred years of Latin-American animosity!

ENDERS: The British are very suspicious about our position.

HAIG (*suddenly angry*): Well, are you surprised? They know where Mrs Kirkpatrick was dining while the invasion was actually taking place!

KIRKPATRICK (*reddening*): That was a long-standing arrangement!

HAIG: You should have postponed it!

REAGAN: Hey, hey, what is all this?

HAIG: While the Argentines were actually storming ashore, shooting and blowing their way into the island, Mrs Kirkpatrick was attending a banquet in her honour at the Argentine Embassy!

KIRKPATRICK (*stung*): That was the only date I happened to be free!

REAGAN: Did you know about the invasion by then?

KIRKPATRICK: Well, yes but –

HAIG: Then you were giving inferential approval!

ENDERS (*laconically*): I was at the dinner too, Mr President. I don't think too much should be read into it.

KIRKPATRICK (*angry now*): If the Argentines *own* those islands, how can the moving-in of their own troops be called aggression?

Everyone winces.

REAGAN (*gently*): I think you should be careful of saying that sort of thing in public, Jean.

ENDERS: Sir, I have a suggestion.

REAGAN: Yes, Tom.

ENDERS: There is oil under those islands. And mineral deposits, rich ones. Surely . . .

KIRKPATRICK (*wearily*): No, Tom.

ENDERS: . . . if we make them agree to split the drilling rights, all this will blow over.

REAGAN: I don't think this is to do with drilling rights.

ENDERS (*genuinely puzzled*): Then why have the British gotten so overheated?

REAGAN: It's pride, it's patriotism, it's because the scars still hurt from loss of Empire . . .

HAIG: It's principle, Tom. The British are nice, reasonable people until someone starts kicking them around, and then they . . . (*He searches for some suitable simile; he gleefully finds it.*) . . . they start behaving exactly like Mrs Kirkpatrick!

REAGAN: All right, all right. (*He tries to draw the discussion to a conclusion.*) I think that the US sympathizes more towards Great Britain on this –

KIRKPATRICK: Mr President –

REAGAN (*irritated*): I said *I* think, Jean. The most practical expression of that sympathy, however, would be impartial US mediation. That's what we offer the British. OK everybody? (*General murmurs of agreement;* JEAN KIRKPATRICK *stays tight-lipped.*) And don't lose any sleep over this – it's just a little scrap over some old bit of sheep pasture.

69. INT. THE 'PRESS CENTRE', MINISTRY OF DEFENCE

A sort of counter at one end of the room, behind which sit NOTT *and* CARRINGTON, *distinctly shaken. Behind them on the wall is a large map of the Falkland Islands. They face strong arc lights and reporters [not seen].* NOTT *is reading a prepared statement.*

NOTT: 'Confirmation has now been received in London that the Argentines have invaded and captured the islands. The Argentine flag flies over Government House, Port Stanley. Diplomatic relations between our two countries have been severed, and a large Naval Task Force is preparing to sail to the South Atlantic on Monday.'

Several reporters [unseen] try to ask questions simultaneously.

REPORTER: Have we declared war?

CARRINGTON: Not yet. But that's a legal point, which will be dealt with by the Law Officers.

REPORTER (*incredulous*): Is the Government seriously planning to settle this dispute by killing people?

CARRINGTON (*hitting the roof*): *We* are not the aggressors! We've called the Security Council into emergency session to settle this peacefully, *we* have! – not the Argentines!

70. INT. THE SECURITY COUNCIL CHAMBER, UN BUILDING, NEW YORK. NIGHT

Pools of light on each delegation round the horseshoe-shaped table.

PARSONS (*forcefully*): I cannot find words strong enough to express my Government's condemnation of this blatant violation of the United Nations Charter and of international law. The Council must act immediately. I propose the following draft resolution:
"The Security Council, deeply disturbed at reports of an invasion by the armed forces of Argentina: 1, demands an immediate cease-fire; 2, demands the immediate withdrawal of all Argentine forces from the Falkland Islands; 3, calls on the Governments of Argentina and the United Kingdom to seek a diplomatic solution of this dispute."

MIX (TIME LAPSE)

COSTA-MENDEZ *at the Argentine delegation's desk, putting on a fine show of righteous indignation.*

COSTA-MENDEZ: The Malvinas are part of Argentine territory, illegally snatched and grabbed by the United Kingdom in 1833 by act of force! Such a criminal act cannot give rise to any rights at all! (*He turns to the black and brown members of the council, appealing to them.*) I call upon all our friends who have ever suffered the cruelties, injustices and ruthlessness of European colonialists – (*he bangs the table in emphasis*) – to reject this imperialist motion, with contempt!

PRESIDENT: There will now be a short recess before the vote is taken.

Instantly, groups form all around the horseshoe-shaped table, as furious last-minute attempts to change and even barter votes are made. It is like the floor of the Stock Exchange during a crisis. PARSONS *and his number two,* HAMILTON WHYTE, *can be seen in the thick of it, persuading, cajoling, arguing.* COSTA-MENDEZ *can be seen noisily arguing with the Russian delegation, who alone have remained in their seats, silent and po-faced.* PARSONS *and* WHYTE *meet up by the British delegation desk again.*

WHYTE (*sotto voce*): Ten votes. Just enough.

PARSONS: It's a damn near-run thing. (PARSONS *spots agitation at the Jordanian desk.*) What's that about?

WHYTE: What?

PARSONS: The Jordanians. They're one of our ten.

WHYTE *starts moving round the central table to find out. At the Argentinian desk,* COSTA-MENDEZ *returns and slumps into his seat, pouring a glass of water.*

COSTA-MENDEZ: I cited non-alignment, anti-imperialism, Argentine grain to Moscow. . . . they'll veto the motion.

ROS: Are you sure?

COSTA-MENDEZ: Certain.

ROS: They said so?

COSTA-MENDEZ: They don't need to.

He drinks. At the British desk, HAMILTON WHYTE *returns, agitated.*

WHYTE: He's just received instructions from Amman to vote against us.

PARSONS: But he's just spoken *for* us!

WHYTE: I know. He's frightfully embarrassed.

PARSONS *glances up at the big clock on the chamber wall, as he snatches up the telephone under the delegation's desk.*

71. INT. THE PRIME MINISTER'S STUDY, 10 DOWNING STREET

MRS THATCHER *is working on her speech for the emergency debate, which is spread out on her desk.* SIR ROBERT ARMSTRONG *(Secretary to the Cabinet) is with her, and has taken the telephone.*

ARMSTRONG: The Foreign Secretary left about ten minutes ago, Sir Anthony. You're in the Security Council chamber *now*?

The PM *takes the telephone from him.*

PM: This is Margaret Thatcher, can *I* help? (*pause*) Yes. Yes I see. (*pause*) The Jordanians. I'll try. (*She clicks the receiver off, and hands handset to* ARMSTRONG.) Will you get me King Hussein?

72. INT. THE SECURITY COUNCIL CHAMBER, UN BUILDING

The hubbub of horse-trading and lobbying is reaching its climax. PARSONS *sits impassively at the British desk, watching the Jordanians. The telephone rings on the Jordanian desk, and* THE AMBASSADOR *answers it. Almost immediately he springs to his feet, and can be seen saying 'Yes, Sir', 'No, Your Majesty', 'No Sir'.* THE PRESIDENT *calls for order.*

PRESIDENT: The vote will now be taken. (*Everyone returns to his seat.* THE JORDANIAN AMBASSADOR *hangs up and turns to talk excitedly to the rest of his delegation.*) Those for the motion?

Eleven put up their hands, including Jordan. PARSONS *visibly says 'phew'.*

WHYTE (*whisper*): The Russians could still veto.

PRESIDENT: Against? (*only Panama.*) Abstentions? (*Poland, Spain, China . . . and Russia.* COSTA-MENDEZ *gawps. There is a hubbub of comment.* PARSONS *allows himself an exhausted smile.*) Resolution 502 is passed.

73. INT. HOUSE OF COMMONS

The emergency debate. MRS THATCHER *rises to the despatch box. She is clearly tired and uncharacteristically nervous, but resolute.*

PM: The House meets this Saturday to respond to a situation of great gravity. For the first time for many years, British sovereign territory has been invaded by a foreign power. The lawful British Government of the Falkland Islands has been usurped. (*resoundingly*) I am sure the whole House joins me in condemning totally this unprovoked aggression by the Government of Argentina against British territory. (*Loud hear, hears! from all sides.*) It has not a shred of justification, and not a scrap of legality! (JUMP-CUT) The Government has now decided that a large Task Force will sail as soon as preparations are complete. HMS *Invincible* will be in the lead, and will sail on Monday. (*Loud approval from both sides.*) Meanwhile, we earnestly hope that our continuing *diplomatic* efforts will meet with success. The Security Council meets again today – (*The opposition laughs.* MRS THATCHER*'s temper momentarily snaps, and she attacks them with scorn.*) Opposition members laugh! They would have been the first to urge a meeting of the Security Council if we had not called one! – they would have been the first to accuse us of sabre-rattling and warmongering! (*She cools down, and concludes*) The people of the Falkland Islands, like the people of the United Kingdom, are an island race. Their way of life is British; their allegiance is to the Crown. They are few in number, but they have the right to *live in peace*, and to *choose* their way of life and their allegiance. It is the wish of the British people, and – (*she smites the despatch box in emphasis*) – and it is the *duty* of Her Majesty's Government, to do everything we can to uphold that right!

She sits, to loud agreement from all sides of the house. FOOT *rises to the despatch box.*

SPEAKER: Mr Michael Foot.

FOOT: The people of the Falkland Islands are faced with an act of naked, unqualified aggression, carried out in the most shameful and disreputable circumstances. (*Hear, hear! all round.*) Any guarantee from this invading force is utterly worthless – as worthless as any of the guarantees that have been given by this same Argentinian fascist junta to its own people. (JUMP-CUT) Even though the position and the circumstances of the people who live in the Falkland Islands are uppermost in our minds – it would be outrageous if that were not the case – there is the longer-term interest to ensure: that foul and brutal aggression does not succeed in our world. If it does, there will be a danger not merely to the Falkland Islands, but to people all over this dangerous planet.

He sits. Loud hear, hears! from all sides. POWELL *rises in the back-benches.*

SPEAKER: Mr Enoch Powell.

POWELL: Mr Speaker. The Prime Minister, shortly after she came to office, received the soubriquet of 'The Iron Lady'. In the next week or two this House, the nation and the Right Honourable Lady herself . . . (*he fixes her with a look of steel across the benches*) . . . will learn of – what – metal – she – is – made.

A murmur goes round the house. MRS THATCHER *is looking directly back at him as he says it, and nods slowly, gravely.*

74. INT. CHAMBER, HOUSE OF COMMONS/DIVISION LOBBIES OUTSIDE/BACK OF SPEAKER'S CHAIR

Members stream out at the end of the debate into the bright spring sunshine, chattering noisily. CARRINGTON *pushes his way through them with determination. His mind is on something else.*

CARRINGTON: Excuse me. Thank you. Thank you.

75. INT. THE ANTE-ROOM TO THE PRIME MINISTER'S ROOM, HOUSE OF COMMONS

Three doors, two large desks with massive typewriters and filing cabinets, a Xerox machine and various hot lines. CARRINGTON *enters from the corridor side.* PYM *and* TEBBIT *are talking. Detectives and two secretaries are present.*

CARRINGTON: Is she in?

PYM: Yes, but pretty shaken.

CARRINGTON: I don't imagine any of us are exactly –

TEBBIT: John Nott's resigned. (CARRINGTON *is startled*) Well, offered his resignation.

PM (*off*): Peter? Is that you?

CARRINGTON *goes through.*

76. INT. THE PRIME MINISTER'S ROOM, HOUSE OF COMMONS

PM: I haven't accepted it. (*She holds up a brief note.*) His department was *not* responsible! This is a time for resolution, not resignation! (*She throws the note down onto the long table, angry, agitated, restless, wanting to hit someone.*) Did you see the end of the debate?

CARRINGTON: The last few minutes.

PM: John attacked the Opposition's defence record.

CARRINGTON (*groans*): Oh Lord.

PM: Lack of commitment to defence spending, lack of patriotism, that sort of thing. You couldn't hear him for howling and jeering.

CARRINGTON: Sit down, I'm going to get you a drink. (*She sits by the fireplace.* CARRINGTON *pours drinks.*) Margaret, someone's got to go. I can't answer back in the Commons, where a Foreign Secretary should be facing the music. (*The* PM *looks up, startled, as she realizes what he means.*) And there's a massive attack on the Foreign Office for not foreseeing this. All three Ministers should go.

He brings her a very weak whisky.

PM: But . . . no one could have foreseen this!

CARRINGTON: My dear, we may be going to war –

PM: Dear God, I hope not. But if we are –

CARRINGTON: – then *some*one's got to lance the boil. In spite of all the loyalty out there (*waves towards Commons chamber*) there's considerable disquiet about how it came about. You can't lead a country to war with that around your neck.

The PM *sips her drink.*

PM: It would be read as disagreement with sending the Task Force.

CARRINGTON: Then I shall make it absolutely clear that I

back that policy one hundred per cent! (*He slaps his palm.*) Up to the hilt!

MRS THATCHER *suddenly looks drained and exhausted.*

PM: Peter, I need you in Cabinet! Please sleep on it.

CARRINGTON *stares into his drink; then shrugs.*

CARRINGTON: Very well.

77. INT. THE PRESIDENT'S STUDY, CASA ROSADA, BUENOS AIRES

ANAYA *and* COSTA-MENDEZ *sit slumped, as* GALTIERI *rages about the room.*

GALTIERI: Would the British send their Fleet eight thousand miles across the world? Not a hope, you said! Ridiculous! Anyhow, they no longer *have* a Fleet! – and the Americans wouldn't let them! – and they couldn't find the way!

ANAYA: It's a negotiating gesture –

GALTIERI: They wouldn't risk an act of nineteenth-century colonial aggression in 1982, you said! World opinion would shout them down! (*He turns savagely on* COSTA MENDEZ.) The *Security Council* would shout them down!

COSTA-MENDEZ: The ways of God are –

GALTIERI (*shouting*): You leave God out of this! He's not a member of the Security Council! And if He was, He'd have voted for Mrs Thatcher too! (*He stumbles into the furniture, and just saves the lamp from crashing to the floor. He steadies himself.*) Well, what do we do? Withdraw? Pull out of the Malvinas, and say sorry? Or do we take on the entire British Navy?

COSTA-MENDEZ *and* ANAYA *do not move for a moment.*

ANAYA (*eventually*): The real question is . . . do you want to stay President?

GALTIERI *slowly turns and looks at him, as the point sinks in.*

78. EXT. BALCONY OF THE CASA ROSADA, BUENOS AIRES. NIGHT.

Guards hastily turn on lights, as GALTIERI *emerges onto the balcony. The square is still quite full, and the people break into cheers. Other members of the junta and senior officials follow, as* GALTIERI *steps forward and flings his arms out, unsteadily.*

GALTIERI (*who has seen Laurence Olivier on the films*): We fight!!

A full-throated roar from the crowd.

79. EXT. GARDENS, CHEVENING PARK, KENT

The official country residence of the British Foreign Secretary. WHITELAW *and* CARRINGTON *gently perambulate in the spring sunshine. The bells of Chevening parish church can be heard in the distance, ringing Grandsire triples.*

WHITELAW: The Argies are ferrying-in huge quantities of men and munitions – tanks, big guns, mines. If we *do* have to attack, a lot of people are going to get killed.

CARRINGTON: I know.

WHITELAW: So it is essential that the Cabinet has people in it who know what fighting is really *like*! Who fought in the War and saw their chaps blown to bits beside them. Who have no illusions about it. Do you realize you and I and Francis are the only ones? (*Silence.* CARRINGTON *makes no response.*) I say, isn't that little fellow lovely. What is he?

CARRINGTON: Er, *Ingwersenianus*, I think, *Cistus Ingwersenianus*.

WHITELAW: Isn't he fine? (*casually, as he examines it*) Did Alec Home ring you up this morning?

CARRINGTON: And Harold Macmillan.

WHITELAW: And Margaret, of course.

CARRINGTON (*laughing*): I knew it was a conspiracy!

WHITELAW: Three Prime Ministers trying to persuade you to stay on! They can't *all* be wrong!

CARRINGTON: You won't shift me, Willy, you cunning old . . . Home Secretary.

WHITELAW *chuckles and ambles on.*

WHITELAW: Just listen to those bells! Sometimes England seems so close, as if you're about to turn a corner and bump into her, putting shit on the roses. (*He chuckles*) Ugly old hag with a wall-eye, I expect. She's not at all easy, always demanding things of you, saying I stand for what I've always stood for and it's what you're here for.

CARRINGTON: *Noblesse oblige*?

WHITELAW: It's more than that. It's recognizing the moment that justifies everything else. Winston said as much, in 1940.

CARRINGTON: You're not seriously comparing this with 1940?!

WHITELAW: In size, of course not. But remember the March into the Rhineland four years before – *that* was about this size. If we had stopped that, there'd have been no Second World War. Just think of that!

CARRINGTON (*quite agitated*): But there is such a thing as Ministerial responsibility!

WHITELAW (*gently*): And there is also such a thing as comradeship, my dear, in times of trouble.

This gets through CARRINGTON'S *defences. He is moved.*

CARRINGTON (*eventually*): Willy, that's *why* I'm going!

WHITELAW *chuckles sadly, gravely, pats his arm in silence, and turns back towards the house.*

80. INT. THE LONG CORRIDOR, 10 DOWNING STREET

Admiral of the Fleet SIR TERENCE LEWIN, *Chief of Defence Staff, comes briskly down the corridor from the front door. He is sixty-two and an immensely nice man – crisp, decisive, irrepressibly cheerful, with a dead-straight, twinkly look. The* PM *and* SIR ROBERT ARMSTRONG *are there to greet him. The* PM *looks a different woman – fresh, confident, energetic and suddenly with an indefinable aura of churchillian relish for the struggle ahead.*

PM: Good morning, good morning, Sir Terence, how splendid to see you back! – have you had any sleep at all?

LEWIN: Enough, Prime Minister, thank you!

PM: You know Sir Robert Armstrong, don't you?

LEWIN: Yes of course, how are you?

ARMSTRONG: Good morning. (*shakes hands.*)

PM: What about some breakfast?

LEWIN: I've done very well, truly!

As she takes him towards the open doors of the cabinet room.

PM: When were you last briefed? Did they bring you up-to-date on the plane?

LEWIN: My team had an hour in the car back from Heathrow to put me straight, and two hours back in the office.

The PM *stops at the Cabinet Room doors.*

PM: I should tell you before we go in – Francis Pym has taken over at the Foreign Office.

LEWIN: I heard that Lord Carrington had resigned.

PM: Yes. (*She gives him a dead pan look*) So now we've got Francis Pym.

81. INT. THE CABINET ROOM

The War Cabinet in session. It looks like a small Cabinet meeting, with only half the chairs occupied.

PM (*briskly*): The War Cabinet will meet every morning at this time – here during the week, and at Chequers at week-ends. We report to the full Cabinet once a week, and when we need their backing for some major decision. That's right, isn't it Robert? We are delighted that the CDS is back. (*Murmur of agreement all round.*) Is there anything you want to say to us at this stage?

LEWIN: Just this, Prime Minister. I think it would be helpful if we could define the Government's objective.

WHITELAW: Objective? (*growl*) 'To win the bloody war.'

PM: Attorney General?

HAVERS: We're not *at* war.

WHITELAW: Of course we're at war!

HAVERS: The Argentines at no stage declared war on us.

WHITELAW: Well, yes, but –

HAVERS (*insisting*): For *us* to do so when we're only reclaiming what was wrested from us by force, would put us on entirely the wrong footing in international law.

WHITELAW (*smiling*): Lawyers' quibbles.

HAVERS: Any action we take would be under Article 51 of the United Nations Charter – the right to armed self-defence.

PM: I think that's perfectly clear. The question of objective . . .

NOTT: Is it simply 'To recapture the Falkland Islands'?

PYM: That's too military. We could still regain them peacefully.

WHITELAW: By economic means, you mean? Sanctions, that sort of thing?

LEWIN: What about 'To cause the withdrawal of the Argentine Forces from the Falklands, by economic, diplomatic and, if necessary, military means, and to restore British administration'. Military last, you see my point.

PYM (*nodding*): A last resort.

PM: I think that states our position. (*general agreement.*) And it brings us immediately to the central decision this morning. (*turning to* NOTT) Secretary of State?

NOTT: Nine major warships have already left the Fleet exercise off Gibraltar, and are steaming to the South Atlantic with all dispatch.

LEWIN *has risen to the map on a large easel at the private office end of the Cabinet table. He indicates positions.*

LEWIN: Here, and here.

NOTT: The two big carriers, *Hermes* and *Invincible*, have been in rapid preparation at Portsmouth throughout the week-end. They sail, with six other warships, if we give the signal . . . (*he glances at the Cabinet clock*) . . . one hour from now. The object would be to do so with maximum, world-wide publicity and tub-thumping – to convince the Argentines we really mean business.

WHITELAW: How long will they take, to get there?

LEWIN: Three weeks.

PYM: Three weeks of increasing pressure to back up the diplomatic offensive.

PM: Precisely, exactly!

HAVERS (*surprised*): Let me get this quite clear, Prime Minister. Are we saying we'll *send* the Task Force, but it won't be used in anger? – only as a diplomatic lever, a tightening of the screw?

WHITELAW: If we send them, there must be no drawing back half-way! – and that means, if diplomatic means fail, we *have* to fight! This must not be another Suez!

PM: That's totally and absolutely right, Willy, exactly the

point! Now do we send those ships? Do we still have the will to resist aggression by force of arms, even half-way around the world, even at huge risk of world opinion turning against us? Because if we *don't* have it any more, for God's sake let's say so now, and pull out before we start! (*She suddenly drops her voice and speaks very quietly.*) It may be we're going to war; people will get killed, innocent people, young soldiers many of whom won't understand what it is they are fighting for. Are we really prepared to do that? Do we still believe what we certainly believed in, in 1940? Or is that now just the romance of history, nothing to do with the cold realities of Britain in 1982, part of a nation that has actually quietly died, as Greece died, as Spain died. Because if in our hearts we secretly believe that *that* Britain is dead, it would be a crime of the direst and blackest sort to send those men to fight – a crime of which the country would very soon find us guilty because their hearts won't be in it, and the first death would light a fuse that would blow us sky-high and clean out of office at the next election! Now – (*briskly, and glancing at the Cabinet clock*) – do we send the signal, or not? Michael?

HAVERS: Yes.

PM: Willy?

WHITELAW: Of course we do.

PM: John?

NOTT: Yes.

PM: Francis?

PYM (*after a pause*): Yes.

82. NEWSFILM

HMS Invincible and Hermes slip their moorings and majestically put to sea, to a cacophony of hooters, sirens and military bands. The quaysides of Portsmouth are packed solidly, as far as the eye can see, with singing, swaying well-wishers waving the Union Jack.

83. INT. THE FOREIGN SECRETARY'S ROOM, FOREIGN OFFICE

FRANCIS PYM *pacing around the magnificent room, dictating a telegram to* A SECRETARY. *He is tough and firm, determined to make the most of the time now gained.*

PYM: I make it my first act as Foreign Secretary to urge the Government of the United States immediately to condemn the invasion, demand the withdrawal of the invader's troops and seek a diplomatic settlement. We have three weeks!

84. INT. THE SECRETARY OF STATE'S ROOM, STATE DEPARTMENT, WASHINGTON

HENDERSON; TOM ENDERS, *who is holding the telegram from Pym; and* HAIG, *who is wandering around, thinking out loud.*

HAIG: I'll tell you what I've been thinking . . . I've been thinking of some sort of *mediating* role for us. You see . . . it might be possible for the US to negotiate with you and the Argentines some sort of mixed administration to run the Islands until –

HENDERSON: We're not going to negotiate anything until the Argies get out!

ENDERS: Isn't that slightly unreasonable?

HAIG (*shaking his head*): Two thousand people on some bleak little rocks at the end of the world . . .

HENDERSON: Remember how all America felt about fifty-two hostages in Iran? And didn't we rush to help you, the moment you asked? (HAIG *and* ENDERS *sit silent; the parallel is just.*) There has been no issue since 1939 on which the British people have felt strongly – right across party lines!

HAIG (*still walking around*): I still see some sort of ... mediating role for someone ...

HENDERSON *flings up his arms and yells in frustration.*

85. INT. THE POPE'S AUDIENCE CHAMBER, THE VATICAN, ROME

THE POPE, *dressed in white, sits on a throne-like wooden chair.* PEREZ DE CUELLAR *sits facing him, in morning dress.*

POPE: You realize I am due to visit Great Britain next month? I cannot go in the middle of a war!

DE CUELLAR: It would look like taking sides.

POPE: Exactly.

DE CUELLAR: But to cancel, your Holiness ...

POPE: Equally taking sides. What would you advise, Mr Secretary-General?

DE CUELLAR (*after thought*): Do nothing at present. Let your decision wait.

POPE: But then all the preparations will go forward! The souvenir-makers will make millions of little plastic Popes ... (*huge despairing gesture*) You will not intervene yourself?

DE CUELLAR: I did intervene. The Argentines ignored me.

POPE (*laconically*): Well, they're Catholics, aren't they? I get that all the time. (*He rises.* DE CUELLAR *rises.*) Keep yourself ready to mediate.

DE CUELLAR: I will, Holiness. At the moment, though, it looks as though the role of mediator may soon be occupied.

POPE: I know. He telephoned me about it. (DE CUELLAR *is startled.* THE POPE *twinkles at him.*) No, not *Him* ... General Haig. You did not know he was a Catholic? (*Musingly, as he leads* DE CUELLAR *towards the door*) He is a formidable man. His only trouble is . . . (*he holds out his ring.* DE CUELLAR *kneels and kisses it.*) . . . his English can sound like my Swahili in bad translation.

86. INT. THE PRESIDENT'S BEDROOM, THE WHITE HOUSE. A CORNER

Close shot of the loudspeaker-telephone beside the bed.

HAIG (*distort*): I could start for London tonight, if this coincides with your crisis perception, Mr President.

Pulling back, we see A VALET *packing clothes for Reagan's forthcoming Caribbean tour. They are distinctly exotic.* REAGAN *is putting out ties and shoes.*

REAGAN: A diplomatic shuttle between London and Buenos Aires? Trying to patch something up?

HAIG (*distort*): That's right, sir.

REAGAN: Like Henry Kissinger used to do?

HAIG (*distort*): Kissinger? Oh yes, yes, but that was different!

REAGAN: Will your heart stand up to it?

87. INT. THE SECRETARY OF STATE'S ROOM, STATE DEPARTMENT

HAIG *on the telephone at his desk. He is as tensed up as the President is relaxed.*

HAIG (*rattled*): Sure, sure, my heart's mach three, nothing whatever wrong with my heart.

REAGAN (*distort*): Anyone who's had – what was it? – triple bypass coronary surgery –

HAIG: Mr President, I'm one hundred per cent fit! One hundred per cent!

REAGAN (*distort*): All right, Al, all right . . .

HAIG: And we've only got seventeen days, OK? Before the British get down there, and a real hot war blows up!

88. INT. HOUSE OF COMMONS

The first full debate of the crisis. JOHN NOTT *is at the despatch box. Gone is any sign of indecision; he speaks with attack and resolve, eyes flashing behind spectacles.*

NOTT: The first action of the Task Force will be to deny the Argentine forces on the Falklands the means of reinforcement and resupply from the mainland. To this end, I must tell the House that the following notice has been promulgated to all shipping today: 'From 0400 GMT on Monday 12 April 1982, a Maritime Exclusion Zone will be established around the Falkland Islands. The outer limit of this zone is a circle of 200 nautical miles from the centre of the islands. From the time indicated, any Argentine warships, submarines or naval auxiliaries found within this zone will be treated as hostile and are liable to be attacked by British forces, without warning.' The force now on the high seas and heading for the South Atlantic, is a formidable one . . .

89. NEWSFILM

Sequence of swooping aerial shots of the mighty ships of the fleet steaming south.

NOTT (*voice over*): . . . There are the carriers of HMS *Invincible* and *Hermes*, with augmented complements of Sea Harriers and Sea-King helicopters; destroyers *Sheffield*, *Glasgow* and *Coventry*, armed with Sea-Dart; destroyers *Antrim* and *Glamorgan* fitted with Sea-Slug; (*We see the energetic preparations of the voyage; practice strikes, helicopter manoeuvres, gunnery practice – a mighty orchestra tuning up.*) frigates *Arrow*, *Alacrity* and *Antelope* with their Exocet surface-to-surface missiles; frigates *Brilliant* and *Broadsword*, with Exocet and Sea-Wolf; frigates *Plymouth* and *Yarmouth* with sonar and helicopters. (*Going in close on the* Hermes *and* Invincible, *cutting majestically through the ocean at top speed.*) When one stops a dictator there are always risks – but there are far greater risks in *not* stopping one – a lesson this country has learned before. (*Camera pans round to show the entire fleet steaming south, a majestic and breathtaking sight. In ringing tones*) Let the world be under no illusion! These people are British, and we mean to defend them! We are in earnest, and no one should doubt our resolve!

END OF PART ONE

INTERVAL

PART TWO

90. LIBRARY FILM

A Boeing 707 wings its way through the skies, a tiny silver speck, high up.

HAIG (*voice over*): Anybody would think it was 1940 all over again! Hitler and Churchill and Their Finest Hour . . .

ENDERS (*voice over*): Argentina is also getting very twitchy, Mr Secretary.

91. INT. HAIG'S PLANE: THE STATE COMPARTMENT. DAY

No more than a partitioned-off section near the front of the plane. HAIG *is in shirt-sleeves, and is tieless.*

HAIG: The more they get excited, the harder it's going to be for us.

GENERAL VERNON WALTERS *comes through from the main cabin, map in hand.*

WALTERS: I've drawn up the 200-mile circle, Mr Secretary. The 'Maritime Exclusion Zone'.

HAIG (*musing over map*): Why the hell couldn't the British have told us about this before we enplaned?

INTERCOM VOICE: Touchdown in twenty five minutes, Mr Secretary.

HAIG *starts putting on tie and jacket.*

HAIG: Neither side *wants* a war. That's our best card.

92. NEWSFILM

Haig's motorcade of sleek black limousines sweeps down Whitehall and into Downing Street.

93. INT. THE CABINET ROOM

The War Cabinet in session, with the Americans. The British sit on the fireplace side, the Americans opposite.

HAIG: One: both sides should withdraw to 500 miles each side of the Falklands. Two: some interim authority should be created on the Islands. Three: the status of the islands should be negotiated by 31 December.

PM: What do you mean, 'status'?

HAIG: Well . . .

PM: Sovereignty?

HAIG: Nothing should be excluded.

PM: You *do* mean sovereignty!

HAIG: I'm trying to de-escalize a war!

PM: So am I! But you do not do so by *appeasement*, you increase its chances!

WALTERS: We're not suggesting app –

PM: You see this table? (*she raps it*) This was where Neville Chamberlain sat in 1938, when he spoke on the wireless about the Czechs as a faraway people about whom we know nothing, and with whom we have so little in common. Munich! Appeasement! A *world war* followed, because of that irresponsible, woolly, indecisive, slipshod attitude – and the deaths of forty-five million people!

The Americans are rattled. They were not expecting this onslaught.

ENDERS: The fact that we have to treat Britain and Argentina even-handedly, for the purpose of negotiation –

PM (*raging*): How dare you treat us even-handedly! Argentina is the *aggressor* and *invader* – a fourth-rate, cruel, unstable, corrupt, brutal regime, with no morals or scruples whatever! They torture and murder their political opponents by the most ghastly Nazi methods . . . and this is the regime you wish to give even a foothold over British citizens?

94. INT. THE SMALL DINING ROOM, 10 DOWNING STREET

A finely-laid table. A BUTLER *is checking each place.* WHITELAW *and* LEWIN *are by the fireplace, in black tie, drinks in hand.*

WHITELAW (*grinning*): The poor chap's head is still spinning.

LEWIN: But did she convince him?

WHITELAW: Difficult to say.

LEWIN: What are our orders for tonight?

WHITELAW: Rattle the Americans; unnerve them! They can't just sit on the fence.

HAIG, ENDERS *and* WALTERS *enter, in lounge suits.*

HAIG: Terry!

LEWIN: Good evening, Al. (*beams and handshakes*) How very good to see you.

HAIG: Hey, how smart you guys look! Tuxedos are the one thing we didn't think to pack. (ENDERS, WALTERS *and the rest of the US team chat to* WHITELAW. *Other members of the War Cabinet drift in –* NOTT, PYM, HAVERS. *To* WAITER.) Give me a soda-water.

LEWIN: How's your heart standing up after that op –

HAIG (*snap*): My heart's fine, fine, absolutely nothing wrong with my heart. Thank you.

He flashes his teeth in an angry smile. The PM *enters, as fresh and full of attack as if it were eight in the morning.*

PM (*big smiles*): Good evening, everybody. Good evening, Al.

HAIG: Good evening, Prime Minister. (*Chorus of good evenings.*) All we were expecting was some sandwiches round the conference table!

PM: Oh, I daresay we'll make you sing for your supper. Besides, I particularly wanted you to see these two portraits

I've had specially moved in here – there we are, aren't they splendid?

HAIG: Er, the Duke of Wellington. Er, Lord Nelson.

PM (*turning on him*): It was their British truculence against another dictator that ensured peace for a hundred years!

HAIG (*heart sinking*): Yes, Prime Minister.

PM (*brightly*): I thought you might like to sit facing them, during dinner.

HAIG (*mutter*): Gee, thanks.

PM: Well . . . shall we de-hungerize?

MIX (TIME LAPSE)

Dinner in progress.

NOTT: The time factor is crucial. There is so little time . . .

HAIG (*nods*): Before the Fleet gets there.

NOTT: No! I mean, the weather!

HAIG (*puzzled*): The weather?

LEWIN: Winter is coming on fast in the South Atlantic. In a very few weeks, conditions will become appalling – fifty-foot waves, and temperatures that never rise above freezing.

WALTERS: Impossible for you to mount the operation?

LEWIN: Exactly.

NOTT: We're certain the Argies hope to string things out until that point is reached. Then we'd have no alternative but to withdraw the Fleet.

WHITELAW: And the entire political initiative would have been lost.

ENDERS (*searchingly*): How do you *know* that's what the Argentines plan?

PM: Wouldn't you, in their place?

ENDERS, HAIG *and* WALTERS *exchange glances, and go on eating. Clearly this is new to them.*

PYM: What precisely are you trying to achieve with this shuttle?

WALTERS: We want to find a line between your needs and the Argentine demands.

PM: Do you support Resolution 502 in the Security Council?

HAIG: Oh absolutely, one hundred per cent!

ENDERS: There'll have to be compromises, Prime Minister. Although the Argentines should not be seen to benefit from the use of force, maybe you should let them keep some kind of . . . residual presence down there.

PM (*angrily*): What?

ENDERS: Mrs Thatcher –

PM: That would just be giving in to them!

HAIG (*irritated*): No way! There would be no itemization of sovereignty.

PM (*astonished*): No itemi – no mention of sovereignty? But that's the central issue! – that and self-determination.

ENDERS: Perhaps we could . . . er . . . . (*waves his hand*) . . . . gently coast round that one.

PM: How on earth could we do that?

HAIG (*vague gesture*): By using a certain constructive ambiguity of wording . . .

PM (*pouncing*): Fudge! – you'd try and fudge it!

ENDERS: The alternative, Mrs Thatcher, is war.

PM (*blazing*): Yes, Mr Enders, it could be, and we don't want war any more than you do, but if the bully-boy marches into your house and starts smashing up the furniture, the first thing you do if he won't stop is throw him out!

PYM (*mutter*): Maybe we should ask the islanders how they feel about that.

The PM *goes white with anger, and turns on him.*

PM: What?

PYM: Before we fight a war in and over Port Stanley, perhaps we should ask the inhabitants if they prefer Argentine rule to annihilation.

PM (*witheringly*): They are British, they have chosen to stay British, they have appealed to us for help, and we are giving it to them *whole-heartedly*! – whole-heartedly, except, that is, for the Foreign Secretary!

Much wincing round the table. PYM *huddles himself up into a silent little lump, and inscrutably continues to eat. Silence.*

ENDERS: Yes, well, it's been a most interesting exchange of opinions.

Silence. Some nervous coughing.

95. EXT. DOOR OF 10 DOWNING STREET

After the dinner party. MRS THATCHER, PYM *and* WHITELAW *waving, as the American motorcade moves off. Policemen salute.*

PM: Goodbye, goodbye! Safe journey!

96. INT. AMBASSADORIAL CAR

WALTERS *and* ENDERS *settle back as they drive away.*

ENDERS: Phew.

WALTERS: I wish there were more like her.

ENDERS: You do?

WALTERS: You know exactly where you stand.

ENDERS (*after thought*): In the corner?

97. INT. THE LONG CORRIDOR 10 DOWNING STREET

The PM *and* WHITELAW *walk back from the front door.* PYM *follows.*

WHITELAW: What do you think?

PM (*doubtful*): Well . . .

WHITELAW: Haig's a brave man. – He's got a string of medals for courage. In Korea, he braved intense enemy fire to blow up his commanding officer's bath-tub, so no Chinese general would get a bath that night!

PM (*acidly*): Wouldn't it have been easier to take the plug? (*a beat.*) No medal then, of course . . .

98. INT. HAIG'S PLANE: THE STATE COMPARTMENT

In flight. HAIG *and* ENDERS, *in shirt-sleeves, either side of the working table, which is covered in drafts. They scribble.* ENDERS *tosses a draft over to* HAIG, *who picks it up and reads it.*

ENDERS: It comes down to those five points.

HAIG (*shaking head*): The Argentines will never accept this! If they did, it would mean the end of Galtieri!

ENDERS: Your best line with him is you're both Generals. He thinks of Generals as a sort of secret brotherhood, running the world.

HAIG: There are Generals and Generals. You know when the Argentine army last fought a war? – (*he leans forward.*) – Eighteen seventy!

99. INT. THE PRESIDENT'S STUDY, CASA ROSADA. NIGHT

It is warm and the windows are open. GALTIERI *is behind his desk, in shirtsleeves.* COSTA-MENDEZ *sits opposite. They have a large file, and are poring over it.*

GALTIERI (*reading*): Hilda – Margaret – Thatcher. Born 13 October 1925. So . . .

COSTA-MENDEZ: She is fifty-seven.

GALTIERI: Husband a . . . 'business-man'? Two children. Father kept a little shop. So where does all this battle spirit come from? (*He passes photographs.*) She is good-looking. It is a pity she is not coming, I could talk to *her*, hohoho. And I could talk to that Foreign Secretary – the Lord, the one who was shot.

COSTA-MENDEZ: Carrington? He was not shot.

GALTIERI: No?

COSTA-MENDEZ: He resigned. In England, there is a distinction.

They look through more photographs.

GALTIERI: Perhaps this Denis is the power. An *éminence grise*, secretly goading her on.

COSTA-MENDEZ (*shaking head*): She is her own woman.

GALTIERI (*huge shrug*): Then I do not understand her!

COSTA-MENDEZ: This is her secret: she has an excellent brain, but the big decisions come from here. (*he taps his breastbone.*) She *knows* what the British people think and feel, and by instinct gives to it a voice – sometimes against all logic. It is a phenomenon more easy to recognize in history than when it is happening. And it is a woman's thing. *That* is the root of her battle spirit – not out of her, but out of that instinct.

A cacophony of motor horns and police sirens can be heard in the distance, getting closer. GALTIERI *continues to turn over the photographs, brooding on them.*

GALTIERI (*muttering to himself*): Holy Mother.

COSTA-MENDEZ (*indicating the noise*): The Americans.

GALTIERI *rises, plucking up his jacket in silence.*

100. ARGENTINE NEWSFILM

Night. Haig's motorcade arriving outside the main gates of the Casa Rosada. The streets are jammed with surging masses of shouting men and women, who appear and disappear into a sea of Argentine flags in a kind of tribal dance. The Argentine flag flutters from every window. Placards and posters ring the square reading: 'Death to Margaret's swine'; 'Goodbye Queen, Long Live Argentina!'; and cartoons of Mrs Thatcher with piratical black patch over one eye. Hundreds of automobile horns blast in rhythm to the crowd's deep-throated roar: 'AR-GEN-TIN-A! AR-GEN-TIN-A!'

101. INT. CORRIDORS/ANTE-ROOMS, CASA ROSADA

Massive Edward VII baroque, in pink marble. HAIG, ENDERS, WALTERS *and the American team being marched by the Argentine* CHEF DIPLOMATIQUE *and his staff, between lines of presidential guards wearing shakos and holding drawn swords at the salute. They turn a corner and come to the impressive double-doors of the presidential study.* GALTIERI *stands there, in full uniform, arms extended.*

GALTIERI (*boom*): General! (*He embraces* HAIG *in a gigantic bear-hug, then holds him out at arm's length by the shoulders.*) Brotherhood among soldiers makes blunt talk good. Haha! (*He thumps* HAIG *on both shoulders.*) Come!

102. INT. PRESIDENT'S STUDY

Standing around the long negotiating table are uniformed representatives of the army and airforce, and a sprinkling of others in civilian clothes. GALTIERI *leads the Americans in.*

GALTIERI (*huge gesture*): These are representatives of the armed forces and the Foreign Ministry. They will be with us as observers.

HAIG: Good evening, gentlemen. (*Chorus of good evenings on both sides.*) Er, which one is Admiral Anaya?

GALTIERI: Admiral Anaya is not present with us.

He gestures the Americans to take a seat at the table.

HAIG: Not present? But I thought – the junta . . . ?

GALTIERI: What need of the junta when you have the President? Hahaha. Be seated.

HAIG *and* ENDERS *exchange glances as everyone sits – wondering if there's been a palace revolution. No junta?*

MIX (TIME LAPSE)

Several hours later. A great deal of whisky consumption in evidence. As we pan round the table –

GALTIERI (*slurred*): We have an internal situation that you will already have felt. Our crisis today can easily result in the destabilization of South America, thereby weakening the defence of the entire West. *That* is why the United States must support us. (*He finishes, and waits for a reply.*)

ENDERS: Perhaps, Sir, you could be more specific.

GALTIERI: You must stop this 'even-handed' approach, and declare your disgust at British Imperialism.

ENDERS: Sir, in the United States, support for Mrs Thatcher is widespread. And the liberal world is overwhelmingly in favour of Great Britain, and would continue to be so if there is war.

GALTIERI: Ha! – there will be no war! That is bluff!

HAIG (*earnestly*): Sir, if you mean that, you never made a bigger mistake in your life!

THE HAWK-FACED OFFICER *on Galtieri's left passes* THE PRESIDENT *a note, which he opens and reads.*

HAIG (*whispers*): Who is that?

WALTERS (*whispers*): Admiral Moya. Could be the junta's front man.

GALTIERI (*resuming*): I must inform you that we have received generous offers of aircraft and armaments from countries *not* of the West! Even last night, I received an urgent, personal letter from Dr Castro.

ENDERS: That's not surprising.

GALTIERI: No?

ENDERS (*pleasantly*): The Soviets are always looking for fall guys, when there's trouble.

GALTIERI *reddens with anger at* ENDERS.

HAIG: What did the letter say?

GALTIERI: It is *very* favourable to Argentina. It would make help from any other country totally unnecessary.

HAIG: Sure, but at what price?

MOYA *leans over and whispers something to* GALTIERI, *who immediately stands.*

GALTIERI: We will adjourn for three hours.

Instantly, all the Argentines stand and break into loud chatter. The Americans are bewildered, HAIG *is angry.*

HAIG: What goes on here? Who's pulling the strings?

WALTERS: Shall we go back to the Embassy? Perhaps you should rest. Your heart . . .

HAIG *gets up with a snarl.*

103. EXT. AMERICAN EMBASSY, BUENOS AIRES. TENNIS COURT

HAIG, *in whites, playing vigorous tennis.* ENDERS *hovers close by.*

HAIG: Who the hell's in operational command around here? (*whack*) How do we get into intercommunicational interaction? (*whack*)

ENDERS: Galtieri –

HAIG: He's the monkey, we want the organ-grinder. Maybe that evil-looking bastard, that Admiral . . .

ENDERS: Moya? (*shakes head*) Costa-Mendez is the one.

HAIG: Yes?

HAIG *stops playing, takes towel from* ENDERS, *starts wiping himself.*

ENDERS: I could draft a compromise position, and try it on him?

HAIG *thinks for a moment.*

HAIG: OK. But they've got to make *real* concessions.

ENDERS: Willie Whitelaw asked me to put the essential difference between the British and Argentines in a nutshell.

HAIG: So what did you say?

ENDERS (*shrug*): 'They're usually drunk, and you're usually sober.'

They start walking briskly back towards the Embassy, Haig still towelling and doing breathing exercises.

HAIG: It's because he's such a simple guy, right out of his depth.

ENDERS: Galtieri?

HAIG (*nods*): Just a peasant, really. Trying to do it all by the seat of his pants – and underneath, absolutely shit-scared. That's why he's alcoholic. (*they walk*) Maybe Costa-Mendez *is* the right road.

ENDERS: Worth trying.

Haig nods.

104. INT. THE PRESIDENT'S STUDY, CASA ROSADA

COSTA-MENDEZ *and advisers on one side of the table;* ENDERS *and his advisers on the other. (Galtieri and Haig not present.) The table is littered with drafts and papers, the atmosphere thick with smoke.* COSTA-MENDEZ *is holding a typed sheet; his advisers crowd round it. The Americans watch.* COSTA-MENDEZ *finally puts the sheet down.*

COSTA-MENDEZ: No.

He passes over a typed draft to ENDERS. *The American team crowd round as they all read it.*

ENDERS (*eventually – icy*): Out of the question!

COSTA-MENDEZ *shrugs and smiles sadly.*

COSTA-MENDEZ: Should we all go home?

ENDERS *suppresses an angry retort.*

ENDERS: Perhaps your General should meet ours. Privately. One last attempt.

105. INT. GALTIERI'S PRIVATE APARTMENT, BUENOS AIRES. NIGHT

Just HAIG *and* GALTIERI, *who is pouring huge tumblers of Glenfiddich. He is still in uniform.*

HAIG: Hey, hey, that's enough!

GALTIERI (*much more relaxed*): Do you not drink? A soldier should drink. The *Russians* can drink, oh ho! – I have never seen so much! You know what they told me? – (*He leans forward and speaks in a stage whisper.*) They will sink the British aircraft carrier, *Invincible*, with Prince Andrew aboard, and let Argentina take the credit! *That* would stop the British!

He leans back, grinning at HAIG'S *astonishment.*

HAIG: How could the Russians do that? Have they got submarines nosing about down there? (GALTIERI *laughs, winks, and taps the side of his nose.* HAIG *continues sharply.*) Look, General. Only soldiers like us can understand just how important it is to avoid conflict. (GALTIERI *turns his bloodshot eyes slowly on* HAIG). You've got to make concessions, real concessions.

GALTIERI (*loftily*): We cannot sacrifice our honour.

HAIG: And I can't be made to look a fool, with the whole world watching, right? So we have common ground.

GALTIERI (*speaking slowly*): If I withdraw from the Malvinas, I would not last one week.

HAIG (*forcefully*): If the British attack, *you would lose*!

GALTIERI: Then I would have to accept military help from whoever offered it.

HAIG: Then you're heading full tilt for a brick wall.

GALTIERI (*almost pleading*): The Americans could order the British to make their Fleet turn back!

HAIG: No! We could not! They'd take no notice! You have my word on that – as a General! (GALTIERI *is slumped. There is no bravado now.* HAIG *speaks quietly, most earnestly.*) Listen. Suppose – suppose you withdrew, but left Argentine flags hanging all over the Falk – er, I mean the Malvinas. Every flagpole, every official building! – and they *have* to stay there, while negotiation takes place, under the UN. (GALTIERI *considers this.*) Now. What would be the result, negotiationwise . . . ?

106. INT. THE PRESIDENT'S STUDY, CASA ROSADA

Montage: a gruelling twelve hours of negotiation between the two full teams. Each side goes into a huddle occasionally to redraft or have a private discussion. Some doze, eat, smoke. The Argentines consume huge quantities of liquor. At one point, ENDERS *leans over to* HAIG.

ENDERS (*quietly*): You know something? We still haven't seen the junta.

HAIG *digests this, unsure how to evaluate it.*

MIX (TIME LAPSE)

Both sides are finally agreed. GALTIERI *and* HAIG *initial a document and stand to shake hands, too exhausted to say anything.*

107. LIBRARY FILM

A Boeing 707 lifts off.

108. INT. HAIG'S PLANE. THE STATE COMPARTMENT. DAY

HAIG *is poring over the initialled document. He is desperately short of sleep.*

HAIG: Hey, this is not so different from the British conceptualization.

ENDERS *fumbles in his pocket and produces a small blue envelope.*

ENDERS: Costa-Mendez gave me this for you. (*He reads the inscription.*) 'Some personal thoughts on our negotiations. Not urgent.'

HAIG *opens it. As he does so –*

HAIG: What day is it?

ENDERS: Sunday. Easter Sunday.

HAIG: By God. So it is. (*He reads, with growing incredulity.*) 'No negotiation without prior guarantee of sovereignty'? 'All British islanders to leave within one week'? (*bewildered*) This is totally opposite to what we've just co-treated! And there's more of it!

ENDERS: What status has that letter?

HAIG: Just 'personal thoughts'. (*explosion of anger*) Of a Class One Screwball, what's he playing at?

WALTERS *comes through from the main cabin.*

WALTERS: Mr Secretary, we have to cable the President in fifteen minutes. And, er . . . (*raising an eyebrow*) . . . His Holiness?

HAIG: Hell yes. Tell them . . . (*he blinks with exhaustion, trying to think.*) 'Proceeding Londonwards. Haig. Happy Easter!'

109. LIBRARY FILM. EXT. ST PETER'S SQUARE, ROME

The huge crowd are gathered excitedly for the Pope's Easter blessing, packing the square as far as the eye can see. The bells of Rome ring and chime from all directions. There is the distant chant of the office.

110. INT. THE POPE'S AUDIENCE CHAMBER, THE VATICAN, ROME

THE POPE'S SECRETARY, *a Jesuit, is reading back a draft of a last-minute addition to the Easter message.* THE POPE *listens, as he is robed, by nuns, for his Easter appearance. The bells are heard through the open doors to the balcony.*

SECRETARY: 'The threatened conflict could lead to dreadful results. We live in a nuclear age, and war, always barbaric, could now lead rapidly to unimaginable consequences for our vulnerable planet.'

POPE: Is it too alarmist?

SECRETARY: The Russians would not hesitate to use nuclear weapons. The Argentines would use them now, if they had them.

POPE: And yet no one should give way to force. The British are right over that.

The white Easter mitre is placed on THE POPE*'s head. He takes the extra page from his secretary, adding it to the rest of his speech, and pats him sadly on the shoulder.*

POPE: Happy Easter.

The huge crozier is placed on his left hand, and he advances to the balcony, followed by his household. The crowd outside is heard to roar as he appears. From behind, we see him blessing them, with huge gesture.

111. EXT. CHEQUERS, EASTER MONDAY, 12 APRIL. DAY

Panoramic shot of the beautiful mellow brick Elizabethan house, set amidst rolling meadow land at the foot of the Chilterns. Lambs gambol about in the spring sunshine; there are great swathes of daffodils. The bells of Ellesborough Church can be heard across the fields, ringing Stedman Surprise caters.

LEWIN (*voice over*): The three nuclear-powered submarines, *Conqueror, Spartan* and *Splendid*, are now well down in the South Atlantic. In fact, *Spartan* has been off the Falklands for some days, undetected. (*Slowly tightening on a big first-floor window of the house.*) Yesterday, she spotted the

Argentine naval landing ship *Cabo San Antonio*, laying mines off Port Stanley harbour. . . .

112. INT. THE GREAT PARLOUR, CHEQUERS

The big, panelled first-floor room, in which the War Cabinet meets at the week-end. It is a light, handsome, peaceful room, with two large windows overlooking green rolling English countryside, and Easter sunshine. There is an alcove at the far end, making the arm of an L-shape. LEWIN *is demonstrating at a large map of the Falkland Islands.*

LEWIN: The Argie ship was here. (*he points.*) *Spartan* radioed Fleet Headquarters in London for permission to attack and sink. This was refused.

WHITELAW (*surprised*): Refused? Why?

PM (*turning to him*): Because we are doing our utmost to achieve a *diplomatic* settlement!

LEWIN: At 4 a.m. this morning, the MEZ came into force – (*he indicates the 200-mile circle round the islands.*) – and *Conqueror* is there to enforce it.

WHITELAW: You call it a Maritime Exclusion Zone – but it's really an old-fashioned blockade, isn't it?

LEWIN: Of a kind. It's to prevent Argentine warships and auxiliaries delivering stores and reinforcements.

WHITELAW: Exactly.

NOTT: Except that it can't be very effective!

WHITELAW: Why not?

NOTT: Because most reinforcements are going in by air. And submarines are not allowed to attack merchant ships by International Law.

HAVERS: It's a reasonable-enough first step. Establish our presence. Opening shot.

PYM: What happens if an Argie merchant ship does try to force its way through?

PM: If the diplomatic offensive is making the *slightest* headway, we turn a blind eye.

LEWIN (*resuming*): *Conqueror* is now heading for South Georgia (*he indicates the route.*) and *Splendid* is operating covertly here – (*he indicates north east of the islands.*) – gathering intelligence. (LEWIN *turns to another map, this one of the whole Atlantic, north to south.*) The main Task Force has begun to assemble here, at Ascension Island, before steaming south. (*he indicates the route from Ascension to the Falklands.*) In two weeks, the main battle group will arrive at the Falklands. The MEZ should then become a *Total* Exclusion Zone. Virtually everything, of any nation, will then be liable to attack without warning, if they venture inside – merchant ships, civil and military aircraft and aircraft on the ground. This is a blockade *plus*, a much tougher tightening of the screw.
The next twist could be the recapture of South Georgia. (*he points*) The one after that, coincident with the TEZ, is the establishment of air and sea superiority, by drawing out Argentine warships and planes and destroying them in battle. This we hope will be completed before the arrival of the Main Landing Force . . .

He indicates a second wave of ships, coming down from Ascension. A momentary chill has gone round the table, at the imminence of hot war.

PYM: But we could halt all this, at any stage?

PM: Absolutely! The moment they realise we're not bluffing! – and they comply with Resolution 502!

HAVERS: Surely they've accepted by now that we're not bluffing!

WHITELAW: I doubt it! I doubt it!

PYM: Al Haig will know.

HAVERS: When does he get back?

PM: Tomorrow morning.

NOTT: With his body-clock in ruins.

113. LIBRARY FILM

A Boeing 707 touches down.

114. INT. THE PRIME MINISTER'S STUDY, 10 DOWNING STREET

The PM, PYM *and* HAIG. *A tray of tea. They all have copies of the document Haig and Galtieri initialled.*

PM: I don't understand the purpose of all these *flags*.

HAIG (*yellow with jet lag*): Oh, that's just a symbol, I think.

PM (*sharply*): Of what?

HAIG: Er, just a face-saver.

PM: No inference about sovereignty?

HAIG (*exhausted*): Over the Falk – I mean, the Malvinas? Sorry, the Falklands?

PYM: I can see one point over which we might shift a little. (*he taps the paper.*) The trauma of invasion may have induced the islanders to soften their previous intransigence.

PM: Over leaseback?

PYM: Over Argentine involvement generally.

SIR ROBERT ARMSTRONG *has quietly entered the room. He now crouches by the* PRIME MINISTER*'s chair, showing her a xerox page and whispering an explanation. She listens, then looks up.*

PM (*to* HAIG): Did you know about this? (*she passes it to him.*) From today's *New York Times*. By Costa-Mendez.

HAIG (*shattered*): This is what he called his private thoughts! – word for word!

PM: Now, it seems, the official policy of Argentina. (HAIG *is enraged.*) Not what you've brought to us, at all!

115. CLOSE SHOT OF A TELEPHONE

HAIG *on the telephone, shouting.*

HAIG: Well what the hell do you mean by it?!

COSTA-MENDEZ (*distort*): It is obvious that the Malvinas must be governed by an Argentine Governor.

HAIG: There was no mention of that in the Agreement!

COSTA-MENDEZ (*distort*): – Oh – that wasn't an Agreement! – just some agreed notes!

HAIG (*with the utmost earnestness*): Dr Costa-Mendez. War is very close. Is Argentina prepared to modify its new position in any way, or is it –

COSTA-MENDEZ (*distort – cheerfully*): But of course!

HAIG (*wearily*): Really?

COSTA-MENDEZ (*distort*): Provided the British will 'decolonize' the Malvinas! – in compliance with the United Nations 1964 Declaration on Decolonization!

116. INT. THE CABINET ROOM

The PM, PYM *and* HAIG, *who is walking around, exploding.*

HAIG (*exasperated*): I've never even heard of it!

PYM: We're trying to find a copy. I must say it doesn't sound very promising.

HAIG: Their entire strategy is prevaricational! But if we're into a war, *they*'d lose!

PM: It still must be followed through, Al. Every avenue.

PYM *produces a couple of folded, typed sheets.*

PYM: Here are our replies to the first Argentine proposals. We can shift on two points – quite a concession, in my view.

HAIG *broods as he glances through it.*

HAIG (*mutter*): Maybe I should go back to Buenos Aires via Washington. Speak with the President.

PM: That's an excellent idea, Al. And you should get some sleep.

HAIG (*twitchy*): I'm fine, fine. I don't need any sleep.

117. LIBRARY FILM

A Boeing 707 lifts off.

118. INT. THE OPERATIONAL CONTROL ROOM, FLEET HEADQUARTERS, NORTHWOOD, N. LONDON

A corner of this highly sophisticated nerve-centre of the British fleet, the 'OCR'. ADMIRAL FIELDHOUSE *is explaining an idea to* LEWIN, *over a map.* FIELDHOUSE *is the Task Force Commander; he is fifty-three, rather Charles Laughton-like, and radiates impenetrable urbanity.*

FIELDHOUSE: The proposal is – one Vulcan bomber – takes off from Ascension, here – with twenty-one thousand-pound bombs on board. She flies four thousand miles to the South Atlantic, drops the bombs and returns. That means seventeen refuelling operations in the air, and fifteen hours of continuous flying.

LEWIN: What do you drop them on?

FIELDHOUSE: Either the runway of Stanley airport – to prevent Argie planes taking off and attacking our Task Force from all directions as it approaches – or here.

He points to the Argentine mainland.

LEWIN: Argentina itself!

FIELDHOUSE: The Argie airfields.

LEWIN: I don't know what the Cabinet will think about *that*.

FIELDHOUSE (*nods*): It's a political decision, certainly.

LEWIN: I'll put it to them. It may well put a bomb under Al Haig.

119. INT. THE OVAL ROOM, THE WHITE HOUSE, WASHINGTON

REAGAN *and* HAIG.

HAIG (*startled*): Galtieri rang you?

REAGAN (*pointing to phone*): Just half an hour ago. Asking me to stop the British Fleet. He sounded desperate.

HAIG: Maybe it's worth one last try.

REAGAN: And another thing. The tide's just starting to turn, in Britain.

HAIG: *I* saw no sign of it!

REAGAN: Like Suez, remember? Play it long enough, and the political will starts to weaken. People start to think – is this *really* just only over some bunch of ice-cold little islands down there?

120. INT. HOUSE OF COMMONS

The house is packed for the third debate on the Falklands crisis. SIR ANTHONY MEYER *is speaking from the back benches.*

MEYER: I have to tell my Right Honourable friends, with great sadness, that I for one am not part of that consensus which believes we should use force if diplomacy fails. (The PRIME MINISTER *swivels on her front bench and watches him intently. The rest of the House remains icily silent.*) I do not believe it would be right to seek out and destroy Argentine vessels, or make an opposed landing – in other words, to kill people – just to ensure that the Union Jack flies over what was left of the public buildings in the Falklands Islands. (*A few isolated but loud hear, hears! from the extreme left, noticeably* WEDGWOOD BENN.) If the Government really intends to carry matters as far as that, I have no doubt they will have the support of this House. Alas, they will no longer have mine.

121. INT. US EMBASSY, BUENOS AIRES

HAIG *doing physical jerks.* ENDERS *is in an armchair, with the Argentine newspapers spread around him on the floor.* HAIG *performs a climactic contortion, and stops, panting, drying himself.*

HAIG: What do the papers say?

ENDERS: They're all dark and full of war fever.

The little clock on the mantelpiece tinkles eleven.

HAIG: I said he wouldn't turn up.

A knock, and WALTERS *enters.*

WALTERS: Dr Costa-Mendez.

COSTA-MENDEZ *enters, very cheerful.*

COSTA-MENDEZ: Good evening, good evening, gentlemen! I have excellent news for you!

HAIG (*wearily*): You have?

COSTA-MENDEZ: It will make all your journeyings worthwhile. (*He chuckles and puts his hand in his breast pocket.*) The junta themselves have drawn up some conditions . . . (*He takes out a completely new document.*) For the ending of hostilities. All points are covered, everything . . .

HAIG: Now wait a minute. What happened to the counter-proposals *we* brought over to *you*?

COSTA-MENDEZ: The British proposals? (*He shakes his head sadly.*) They were rejected.

HAIG: *Totally*?

COSTA-MENDEZ: They were not very realistic, you know.

ENDERS *has been scanning the new document. His blood boils.*

ENDERS: They want shared administrative control. Provision for saturating the islands with Argentinians to push out the existing population . . . (*He folds the document carefully and hands it back, speaking very courteously.*) I think, Dr Costa-Mendez, that you should go boil your head.

HAIG: The British will shoot when they get that.

COSTA-MENDEZ *is shaken.*

COSTA-MENDEZ: You are serious?

ENDERS (*charmingly*): No no, we often fly back and forth across the Atlantic without sleep, day in, day out, just for the hell of it.

HAIG *is keeping his temper with great difficulty.*

HAIG: I shall fly to Washington tomorrow, and tell the President that there is absolutely no point in continuing my mission. British military action is imminent!

COSTA-MENDEZ (*flustered*): My advice . . . my advice is to speak to the junta first.

HAIG (*Sudden howl*): *That* is what I have been *trying* to do for *ten days*!!

COSTA-MENDEZ: Well, I will – I will see what, er, can be arranged. Excuse me.

He scuttles out. HAIG *immediately snatches up the telephone.*

HAIG: I want you to get me right through to Number One. Right away, OK?

He hangs up.

ENDERS: Is that wise?

HAIG: Why not?

ENDERS: That line is sure to be bugged.

HAIG (*hissing*): Exactly! (*The telephone buzzes,* HAIG

answers.) Hallo. Yes, yes. Right. (*pause*) Hallo, Mr President? Not good, no. (*pause*) It would be pointless to carry these latest proposals back to London. Admiral Lewin would just decimate the Argentine Fleet out of the water. And they'd drop those atom bombs on all the mainland airports, we couldn't stop them . . . Unless I met the junta, yes, of course.

122. INT. CORRIDORS/ANTE-ROOMS CASA ROSADA. DAY

HAIG, ENDERS, WALTERS *and the Americans being lead between lines of presidential guards as before.* COSTA-MENDEZ *is accompanying them.*

COSTA-MENDEZ: It was the most extraordinary good luck that I managed to contact all members at such short notice . . . extremely fortunate that they could convene, well, overnight, amazing . . .

They turn a corner and come to the impressive double-doors of the presidential study. The doors are open. Beyond them stand the three members of THE JUNTA, *in full uniform, stiffly to attention. It is an eerie sight, and* HAIG *pauses in his tracks with suppressed exclamation.*

123. INT. THE PRESIDENT'S STUDY, CASA ROSADA

THE JUNTA, *backed by* ADVISERS *and* SECRETARIES, *sit on one side of a marble-topped conference table;* THE AMERICANS *are on the other.* HAIG *has dragged up the last reserves of his energy for a semblance of brisk attack, to lay it on the line.*

HAIG: One. The United States Government could not see two friends at war. Two. Britain is not bluffing, and Washington would not tolerate the fall of the Thatcher Government.

Therefore: Argentina *has* to enter realistic negotiations on the basis of Security Council Resolution 502, *now*, today, or . . . (*He leans forward to emphasize*) *America will side with Britain*. Be in no doubt about that. I have the President's authority for saying that. You know how close the British Fleet now is. Unless there is a radical change in Argentina's position, there's going to be a hot, shooting war in your laps almost immediately.

An uncomfortable pause.

ANAYA: If Mrs Thatcher's stubbornness –

HAIG (*brisk*): It's not her stubbornness. It's yours.

ANAYA *flushes with annoyance. He leans forward and speaks with icy steadiness.*

ANAYA: My son is a helicopter pilot. He is ready to die for the Malvinas. My family would be proud to know his blood had been mixed with that sacred soil.

HAIG (*equally steady*): That's the sort of talk that stops, when you see the remains of young men being shovelled into body bags. (*He leans across the table, pointing at him.*) Which *you* have never seen.

GALTIERI (*threateningly*): If the British attacked, Port Stanley would be annihilated. Its buildings are made of wood – most of the inhabitants would be burned to death – women and children . . .

WALTERS (*with cold fury*): I wonder why they're still there, General? My information is they have been forced to stay!

DOZO *has not so far spoken. An untidy, intelligent man like an Argentine Nicko Henderson, he now speaks quietly.*

DOZO: It is vital that both Argentina and Britain withdraw before negotiation. That is clear. (GALTIERI *and* ANAYA *indicate strong dissent.*) But there is nothing to prevent us saying that *we* demanded that.

HAIG (*after a pause*): What?

DOZO: That Argentina insisted on withdrawal by both sides. To show our complete confidence of the outcome.

HAIG *almost gawps at him.* GALTIERI *thinks quickly.*

GALTIERI (*casually*): That could be in writing? In the treaty?

ENDERS: Why not?

GALTIERI *throws back his head, and gives* ANAYA *a look of Caesarian authority.*

GALTIERI: I agree.

ANAYA (*murmur*): You see? We are not so far apart.

ENDERS, WALTERS *and* HAIG *are incredulous. But they take a grip on themselves, in spite of fatigue, and prepare to negotiate once more.*

124. MONTAGE

Ten hours of haggling, drafting and redrafting. Both sides separate, confer among themselves, return to the table; grow angry, pound the table, snatch sleep on benches and sofas. Finally a document of sorts is agreed, and typed up. Like sleep-walkers, both sides sign and shake hands mechanically.

125. LIBRARY FILM

A Boeing 707 lifts off as if it itself were exhausted.

126. INT. HAIG'S PLANE. THE STATE COMPARTMENT. DAY

HAIG, ENDERS *and* WALTERS, *pole-axed by exhaustion, flick through the new agreement..*

HAIG (*mutter*): It will be a miracle if she agrees to this.

AN AIDE *comes through from the main cabin.*

AIDE: Mr Secretary. Sir. Pardon me. I was given this for you, just as we took off.

He produces a familiar blue envelope. HAIG *stares at it, as if turned to stone.*

HAIG: By Dr Costa-Mendez.

AIDE: Yes sir.

HAIG: His private thoughts on our negotiations. Not urgent.

AIDE: Yes, sir.

HAIG *takes it.* THE AIDE *disappears.* HAIG *cannot open it. He hands it to* ENDERS. ENDERS *opens it and reads.*

ENDERS: It goes back on everything. (*He crumples it up. They sit there, their souls turned to lead.*) My conscience is clear. So should yours be.

HAIG (*barely audible, and close to tears*): I'm just thinking of all those body bags.

127. LIBRARY FILM

Haig's plane seen high up, a tiny silver speck in the sky.

128. INT. THE CABINET ROOM

The War Cabinet in session: the PM, NOTT, PYM, WHITELAW, HAVERS, ARMSTRONG *and* LEWIN.

WHITELAW: If Haig won't call a halt now, *we* should!

PYM: That would be a mistake.

WHITELAW (*angry*): Why would it be a mistake?

PYM: *We* must not be seen to abandon negotiation.

WHITELAW: But we can't just go on talking for ever! – clearly they have no intention of acting in good faith.

NOTT: And the weather down there is deteriorating rapidly, Prime Minister.

WHITELAW: Ah-ha, yes! Exactly!

PM (*to* LEWIN): How long before the first ship gets to the MEZ?

LEWIN: Six days, Prime Minister.

PM: If the Haig mission *has* ground to a halt, the Americans should say so; they should come down publicly on our side, and the UN must take over negotiations immediately. Time is *not* on our side. (*General agreement from all.*) Francis should fly over tonight and set all this in motion.

PYM: It could be done by telepho –

PM (*ploughing on*): Confront Haig face-to-face and demand to know whether you or he should take it to the United Nations.

PYM: Do you think it's wise to leave my desk just when –

PM (*flatly):* Yes. (*to* ARMSTRONG) Yes?

ARMSTRONG: Rules of Engagement.

PM: Admiral Lewin?

LEWIN: Prime Minister, the war cabinet will be aware that the Royal Navy has always issued sets of instructions to its captains about the circumstances in which they can fire on the enemy. Normally, they are based on the principle of self-defence; but as the Task Force nears its objective, the rules will need to be changed, as is normal in warfare.

PYM: We're not yet *in* warfare.

PM (*brushing this aside*): Do you have particular circumstances in mind?

LEWIN: Yes. Yesterday, Argentine Air Force Boeing 707s started to shadow the Task Force. They were identified by Sea Harriers. Admiral Woodward requests permission to shoot them down.

Several members are shocked.

PYM: How are these planes armed?

LEWIN: They are unarmed, but –

WHITELAW (*appalled*): But that would be intolerable!

LEWIN (*patiently*): If I may finish, Prime Minister. They are reconnaissance aircraft. Their job is to vector Argentine submarines and strike aircraft onto the track of the Task Force. One or both our aircraft carriers could be sunk, without our having fired a shot, and we'd have lost the war. *That*'s the danger.

Pause. The realities of this, the first real military decision, shake many present.

WHITELAW: Prime Minister, such permission should surely be limited to when the Task Force enters the MEZ! To shoot them down on the high seas, without warning . . .

He shakes his head, appalled.

LEWIN: No one is suggesting they should not be warned.

PYM: Even so . . .

PM: We are trying to achieve a *diplomatic* settlement.

PYM: Hear, hear!

LEWIN: I should like no one to be in any doubt about the risks involved.

PYM: The alternative is unthinkable.

PM: Agreed? (*Nods and mumbles all round.*) Next?

ARMSTRONG: South Georgia.

PM: Ah yes. The main question this morning is whether we mount an operation against South Georgia before the main landing on the Falklands themselves. CDS?

LEWIN *has crossed to the easel. The map shows South Georgia and the Falklands.*

LEWIN: South Georgia is eight hundred miles from the primary objective. Strategically, it is largely irrelevant to the retaking of the Falklands, and will probably be surrendered automatically when they've been taken. The island is mountainous and covered with glaciers. Weather conditions are pretty foul at this time of the year – heavy snow and gale force winds . . . (*He has removed the map to disclose a series of photographs of the island – bleak, craggy icy wastes.*) If an action to retake should fail, or there is substantial loss of life, it would be a devastating prelude to the main campaign. Having said that, the ships and manpower *are* available, and we believe the island could be recaptured without diverting effort from the main objective.

PM: Minister of Defence?

NOTT: It's more than two weeks since the Task Force sailed. Buenos Aires remains intransigent. The public is becoming restless for *some* action that will keep the political will going. In my view, we should go in.

PM: Home Secretary?

WHITELAW: I think that's right. One short, sharp action would put ginger into the negotiations as they pass to the UN. We should go ahead.

PYM: Whatever the weather?

The PM *turns and looks at him, without answering.*

129. NEWSFILM

Appalling conditions at sea. British ships just glimpsed through blizzard and Arctic seas.

130. INT. HAIG'S OFFICE, STATE DEPARTMENT, WASHINGTON

HENDERSON *is with* HAIG, *who is considerably shocked and agitated.*

HAIG: You're bound to casualtize, you can't help but casualtize!

HENDERSON: Al –

HAIG: You listen to me for a moment –

HENDERSON (*insisting*): It would be *saving* life, don't you see, if Buenos Aires is shocked into sense by one small landing, without our having to invade the Falklands themselves!

HAIG (*muttering*): I see that. I see that.

HENDERSON: But does your President?

HAIG: We're trying to isolate him from all this . . .

HENDERSON: Isolate?!

HAIG: And failing one hundred per cent! Every time he turns on his TV, he tells me, there's (*bleep*) Nicko Henderson, saying Hurrah for Britain all over again!

131. INT. THE OVAL ROOM, THE WHITE HOUSE, WASHINGTON. DAY

Close shot of a television screen. HENDERSON, *with wayward silver hair and crumpled, elegant suit, is being interviewed. He is a natural, and all America is entranced.*

HENDERSON: As far as I know, there has been no estimate of costs, if we have to start fighting.

INTERVIEWER: Isn't that rather naïve, Sir Nicholas?

HENDERSON: No, sir, it is not! – (*pulling back.* REAGAN *sits watching, on a sofa at the fireplace end of the room. He is in dressing-gown and is drinking his morning coffee.*) Remember that the British spent the accumulated wealth of an entire century fighting two World Wars! – defending the cause of freedom of the individual, and democracy. Were we wrong to do that? (*He leans forward, with the utmost courtesy.*) We had to wait for you from 1914 to 1917, and 1939 to 1942. How long shall we have to wait for you now?

REAGAN (*groaning to himself*): Oh boy.

132. LIBRARY FILM

The sleek, black, Prime Ministerial limousine sweeps through the streets of north London, heading north. A smaller, heavily-armed security car precedes it, and another follows.

NOTT (*voice over*): Did you see the weather reports from South Georgia?

PM (*voice over*): Yes . . .

NOTT (*voice over*): Sea conditions aren't much better.

133. INT. PM'S CAR

The PM *and* NOTT, *going through signals and telegrams. Their red boxes lie open on the seats beside and in front of them.*

NOTT (*continuing*): Force six gales and flurries of snow. And a lot of icebergs – *Conqueror* reports one thirty-five miles by twelve.

PM: Have you seen number 418? Galtieri is actually on the Falklands at the moment.

NOTT: Giving pep talks to his troops. (*leafs through to another one.*) 'The British may defeat us, but they cannot break our spirits.'

PM (*surprised*): He said that? About defeat?

NOTT: Number 302. (*The* PM *finds her copy, and studies it thoughtfully.*) Here we are.

134. EXT. FLEET HEADQUARTERS, NORTHWOOD, N. LONDON

Security stricter than any prison surrounds the giant granite and glass office complex. It is dominated by huge radio antennae and discs. There is a great deal of stamping and saluting and raising of successive barriers, as the PM's motorcade enters the highly-guarded and defended perimeter of the complex. The two escort cars peel off, and the PM's own car drives through the main office blocks to turn down a side road. Immediately the scenery changes, becoming much bleaker and bare of trees. Suddenly, there, ahead, looms an awesome sight: every child's idea of the visible part of a nuclear bunker. A massive, windowless concrete structure, about the size of Hawksmoor's mausoleum at Castle Howard, and with something of the same grey timelessness and monumentality in an empty landscape. It is surrounded by three successive twelve-foot high barbed wire fences, one inside the other, and a bare no-man's-land, presumably heavily mined. The PM's car sweeps towards it.

135. INT. 'THE HOLE', NORTHWOOD

The PM *and* NOTT *being led down steep narrow stairs by* ADMIRAL SIR JOHN FIELDHOUSE *and senior officers from all three services. The ceilings are crammed with cables and pipes of all sizes, making it feel like the corridors of a ship. At each turn of the stairs are immensely thick nuclear-blast doorways, like strong-room doors, standing open.*

FIELDHOUSE: We've just heard from the *Antrim*. The SAS helicopters are taking off at the moment.

PM: Can you speak direct to the ship?

FIELDHOUSE: Oh yes, Prime Minister.

(JUMP-CUT: COMING DOWN NEXT FLIG[illegible] STAIRS.)

NOTT: What's the weather like?

FIELDHOUSE (*very calm and* [illegible] lence. Fifteen degrees [illegible] oeuvring on pitchi[illegible]

PM (*worried*): Sh[illegible]

FIELDHOUSE: Oh no, Prime Minister. If we did, the weather might become unpleasant.

136. INT. OCR, FLEET HEADQUARTERS, NORTHWOOD

The top-secret underground control room, deep in the heart of the bunker, from which all fleet and submarine movements are directed in time of war. It is built like a hexagonal miniature theatre. On the 'stage' position, large maps are either projected or hung, vertically. Wrens push magnetic markers about with long wands, each one indicating a ship or squad of troops or aircraft paths. In the 'stalls' area are two banks of consoles not unlike a television studio control room suite. On them stand small green-screened VDUs with keyboards and other apparatus beneath. Each one is manned. These are the signals input and output points, which are in continual use direct to individual ships and submarines, via satellite.

FIELDHOUSE *conducts the* PM, NOTT *and senior officers into the small balcony in the 'circle' area. There are his desk, map tables, duplicates of some of the main screens. The whole operation in the main theatre below may be seen with ease from this position.* FIELDHOUSE *is explaining the big map of South Georgia below, using a tiny light-spot indicator to point out markers.*

FIELDHOUSE: The *Antrim* is there, Prime Minister. *Plymouth* there. The tanker *Tidespring* is moving up here, and *Endur-*
here. (*Wrens are continually adjusting the position of*
hey receive location-signals. Each marker
f the vessel mounted on a metal plate.)
ers have just taken off from *Antrim*
AS mountain troops on Fortuna
at the moment, crossing
p helicopters are tak-
ytvikin, here.

PM: Are the red markers the Argentine positions?

FIELDHOUSE: No, Prime Minister, Argentine radar beam markers. We *think* the enemy is here and here – (*he indicates Leith and Grytvikin.*) – but the submarine *Conqueror* did a periscope recce yesterday along the north coast, and couldn't spot them.

NOTT: There are about a hundred and twenty Argentine marines on the island, we know that.

FIELDHOUSE *hands over several blow-up aerial survey photographs.*

FIELDHOUSE: These were taken at dawn today, and transmitted by satellite. You can see the terrain . . . (*The* PM *leafs through them – rocky, icy, barren mountainous wastes seen from dizzying height.* A WREN *has come up with a further batch of signal print-outs.* FIELDHOUSE *murmurs.*) Excuse me, Prime Minister.

He leafs through them. He is clearly worried.

NOTT: Anything significant?

FIELDHOUSE (*casually*): The weather isn't improving.

PM: Can you speak direct to the *Antrim* about that? I'm very worried about conditions.

FIELDHOUSE *leans back to his desk and picks up an ordinary-looking grey telephone. A small notice is propped against it reading 'Task Force Commander Only'.*

FIELDHOUSE: Hallo, Brian? The Prime Minister is with me. How's the weather looking outside your window? (NOTT *and the* PM *are astonished at the simplicity of this direct line.*) He says he lost sight of the helicopters as they disappeared into the snow. He could see them for the first two hundred yards.

PM: Should we postpone the operation? Is it simply too awful?

FIELDHOUSE (*on telephone*): Hallo Brian? Will the SAS be able to operate? (*pause as he listens*) He says it'll be OK if they can camp overnight. They've got tents. The problem is pitching them in a blizzard.

He hangs up. The PM *is plainly both shocked and impressed by what she has just heard.*

NOTT: Could we not stay listening in?

FIELDHOUSE: I'd prefer not, if you don't mind. We've got to leave them to make their own judgements – and if you start listening in, the temptation is to start interfering.

NOTT *nods. He is almost biting his nails with tension. The contrast between the calm professionalism of the OCR and the tempestuous operation going on eight thousand miles away, is eerie.* A WREN *brings up a signal on different coloured paper.* FIELDHOUSE *reads it, hands it to the* PM.

PM (*with signal*): The *Veinticinco de Mayo* . . .

FIELDHOUSE: It's altered course. Northwards.

NOTT: *Away* from the Falklands?

FIELDHOUSE: Towards our approaching Task Force. (*casually*) It could mean nothing, of course.

137. INT. CORRIDORS/ANTE-ROOMS CASA ROSADA. DAY

The doors of the President's study burst open, and ANAYA *emerges rapidly, followed by* GALTIERI. *It is clear they have been having an almighty row.*

GALTIERI: It is customary to *tell* your President!

ANAYA (*striding along*): I thought a signal had been sent to you.

GALTIERI (*half-running beside him*): Oh, it *was*! – by Russian military intelligence! Kind of the Russians, don't you think, to let me know when you deploy the biggest ship in the Argentine Navy! *Why* is she heading north?

ANAYA: The plan is flexible.

GALTIERI: Ah, flexible, yes of course, wonderful. You are not by any chance thinking of attacking the British Task Force as it –

ANAYA (*stopping*): Listen, Leopoldo! The weather, the *weather*, will defeat Margaret Thatcher! You have everything you want!

He strides off. GALTIERI *shouts after him.*

GALTIERI (*roar*): Oh no I haven't! I want someone I can *trust* to run the Navy! – like Admiral Lewin!

138. INT. THE SECRETARY OF STATE'S ROOM, STATE DEPARTMENT, WASHINGTON

PYM *and* HAIG, *breakfasting –* PYM *on bacon and eggs,* HAIG *on fruit juice.*

PYM (*tucking in*): If there's to be any sort of bridge with Britain's bottom-line principles –

HAIG: The package on the table, Francis, is Haig Two.

PYM (*looking up*): I beg your pardon?

HAIG (*blushing*): I know, it's kinda embarrassing. But that's what my officials keep calling it.

PYM: Well . . . we think the time has come to take 'Haig Two' to the United Nations –

HAIG: Francis! Argentina is falling into chaos by the hour! Inflation is two hundred per cent, there's rioting and looting and . . . It's too *late* for all that!

139. INT. THE CABINET ROOM

The PM *and* ARMSTRONG, *with draft agenda for Thursday's cabinet. The* PM*'s thoughts are elsewhere.*

ARMSTRONG (*indicating*): . . . the fourth item will be the

Foreign Secretary's report on his meeting with Haig. There will be a paper to go with that.

PM: Mm? Yes, there will be, of course.

ARMSTRONG *quietly registers that the* PM *is only half listening.*

ARMSTRONG (*putting papers away*): The rest of the agenda is straightforward.

PM: Were you ever in the forces, Robert?

ARMSTRONG (*little glance*): No.

PM: We saw very little of the real war when I was a child. There was *some* bombing in Grantham, and I suppose some people were . . . I suppose there were casualties. I don't remember.

Silence. Then the telephone buzzes. ARMSTRONG *answers it.*

ARMSTRONG: Yes? (*listens*) Can Admiral Lewin see you?

PM: Of course.

ARMSTRONG: Yes please.

He hangs up, and LEWIN *enters immediately.*

LEWIN: Good morning, Prime Minister.

PM: Please stay, Robert.

LEWIN: Those Wessex Five helicopters . . . Can I show you over here? (*He leads the way to a side-table at the St James's Park end, where a large map of South Georgia is laid out. Beside it are the aerial photographs from Northwood. He points.*) Here's where they landed last night. They tried to pitch tents, but they were largely blown away. The temperature dropped to minus forty and there was a gale with a hundred-mile-an-hour gusts during the night. (*Tightening on the aerial photographs, showing the Arctic conditions.*) This morning they radioed for immediate rescue. The two helicopters that went out to get them in the blizzard overturned and crashed, one full of men it had just rescued – about here.

The PM *stands as if frozen. Her grief is evident, and she begins to weep silently.*

ARMSTRONG (*quietly*): Casualties?

LEWIN: We don't know. The whole operation's been aborted while they try and get them out . . .

Close shot of the recce photos. Arctic gales heard over. Mix to –

140. INT. THE PM'S STUDY, 10 DOWNING STREET. NIGHT

Low lighting, 4 a.m. The PM *is asleep in an armchair, fully clothed. Open red boxes are by her. We pan over the framed photographs of her family by the boxes – father, mother, husband, son, daughter; wedding photograph; first day as a young MP; and holding the twins when babies, one in each arm. The telephone buzzes. She wakes, answers it.*

PM: Yes?

VOICE (*distort*): Will you speak to the CDS, Prime Minister?

PM: Yes, of course.

LEWIN (*distort*): I'm sorry to wake you at this hour.

PM: Have those men been found?

LEWIN (*distort*): Yes.

PM: Thank God!

LEWIN (*distort*): They've got frostbite and hypothermia but they're all alive.

141. INT. OCR, FLEET HEADQUARTERS, NORTHWOOD

On the 'balcony'. LEWIN *on the telephone. The room is in action below him.*

LEWIN (*continuing*): But the weather's got worse and I'm afraid the second attempt to land has had to be aborted as well. Some men have been swept out to sea.

142. CROSS-CUT OCR/PM'S STUDY

LEWIN (*continuing*): An enemy C-130 reconnaissance plane has been low-flying over our ships, and we've picked up signals from one of their submarines. Fieldhouse has ordered our ships to scatter.

PM: Because of the submarine?

LEWIN: And the long-range bombers, which the plane could be vectoring out from the mainland.

PM: Couldn't we shoot it down?!

LEWIN: Easily! But the Rules of Engagement don't allow it.

PM: Then the main assault . . . ?

LEWIN: We'll have to review that when the sub's been located, Prime Minister. If we can find it.

143. NEWSFILM

Appalling Arctic seas crash down on the decks of the Antrim *and the* Endurance.

144. INT. THE PRIME MINISTER'S STUDY, 10 DOWNING STREET

WHITELAW *with the* PM, *who is walking about in a state of considerable agitation and emotion.*

PM: It's a terrible thing to send men in to fight, to risk their young lives in those . . . *atrocious* conditions!

WHITELAW: They're professionals!

PM: Of course they are, and superb, but . . . I've never *seen* fighting, Willy.

WHITELAW: You'd be even more certain about what you're doing, if you had.

She barely hears him, as she walks about.

145. INT. OCR, FLEET HEADQUARTERS, NORTHWOOD

Close shot of a VDU screen, like a small television set. A signal flashes up on it: 'Wessex III to Antrim flash copy CINC fleet. Goblin on surface range 4500 bearing 315 am attacking. Flash 252141 Out'. THE WREN *operating this VDU instantly presses the print-out button. Two copies, like telexes, jump out. She snatches them up and runs down the banks of consoles to* FIELDHOUSE, *handing one copy to the Wrens operating the big display map of South Georgia as she passes.*

FIELDHOUSE (*calling to Lewin*): They've found the sub. On the surface.

LEWIN *runs over, as* FIELDHOUSE *finds the position on his table map, plotting it with great care.*

LEWIN: Here, heading like this. It's well within the twenty-five miles Rules of Engagement radius – it's less than a mile from *Endurance*!

FIELDHOUSE *snatches up the 'growler' (or the direct satellite secure-voice [DSSS] link) to the South Atlantic.*

FIELDHOUSE: Brian?

YOUNG (*distort*): Hallo, sir! – I've just sent you a second flash.

In the background of the growler transmission can be heard the garbled voices of the helicopter pilots talking back to base ship.

FIELDHOUSE: What is she doing on the surface?

YOUNG (*distort*): Dropping reinforcements on the island, we think sir. I've vectored up the two Wasps to support Wessex's attack.

A WREN *runs up with the second signal which reads: 'I SS position 86470283 course 030 speed 8 attacking with two MARK IX then WASP AS.12. Flash* Antrim *to CINC fleet 252145'. The judder of helicopter blades and voices of the pilots can be heard over the growler.*

PILOT (*faint – distort*): Dropping to one hundred, one hundred, closing at one fifty . . .

YOUNG (*distort*): They're engaging now!

146. INT. THE CABINET ROOM

LEWIN *addresses the War Cabinet, standing at the easel. He is urgent and forceful.*

LEWIN: The helicopters attacked with Mark XI depth-charges and torpedoes from this direction. HMS *Plymouth*'s Wasp fired an AS.12 missile, which passed right through the conning-tower, while HMS *Brilliant*'s Lynx closed in firing its machine-guns. It's amazing the sub remained afloat. It was severely damaged and beached near Grytvikin, here. (*He points.*) The crew jumped into the water and could be seen running along the coastline here, looking for cover. (*Demonstrating.*) Major Sheridan is preparing to storm ashore with such men as he can immediately muster, and attack while they are disorganized.

PM: Where is the official landing force?

LEWIN: Right out here – (*he points to a spot a hundred and fifty miles from the islands.*) – on the *Tidespring*. She went out there when Fieldhouse ordered the ships to scatter.

WHITELAW: How many men can Sheridan muster?

LEWIN: Seventy-five.

NOTT: Against how many?

LEWIN: We don't know. *Antrim* and *Plymouth* would bombard suspected enemy positions (*pointing*) here and here, and the assault would go in at 2.45 this afternoon.

HAVERS: Bombard?

LEWIN: They have four-point-five guns. They would sail across the bay in a wide arc, like this. (*he indicates.*)

HAVERS: While firing?

LEWIN: Exactly. Strictly military targets.

NOTT: Isn't it, well, a bit of a gamble?

LEWIN: Of course it's a gamble! It would be a bigger gamble to do nothing!

PM (*To War Cabinet.*): Agreed?

147. INT. OCR, FLEET HEADQUARTERS, NORTHWOOD

On the 'balcony' FIELDHOUSE *has the growler telephone. He switches on the telephone loudspeaker on his desk. The bombardment is heard to commence, with eerie booms, eight thousand miles away. One by one, the personnel in the OCR stop and quietly listen to this strange and haunting sound.*

148. INT. THE 'PRESS CENTRE', MINISTRY OF DEFENCE

IAN MACDONALD *intones straight to us, on camera, sepulchrally.*

MACDONALD: At ten o'clock this morning – the Argentine garrison commander – surrendered. (*Mournfully*) Troops from the SBS – previously listed missing – have been rescued. No lives were lost in the operation.

UNSEEN REPORTER: So we *won*?! We've retaken South Georgia?!

MACDONALD *considers this highly suspicious question for a moment. Eventually –*

MACDONALD (*funereally*): Yes.

149. INT. THE PRIME MINISTER'S STUDY, 10 DOWNING STREET

JOHN NOTT *has just read out the surrender signal to the* PRIME MINISTER, *who is almost speechless with relief.*

PM: Could we go outside and read the wording of the signal to the Press? – no loss of life!

NOTT: They may ask some pretty silly questions.

The PM *hits the roof in a sudden explosion of relief, joy and contempt.*

PM: Oh! – tell them to *rejoice*! – just rejoice!

150. INT. HOUSE OF COMMONS

MRS THATCHER *at the despatch box, finishing her statement.*

PM: . . . About a hundred and eighty prisoners were taken, including up to fifty military reinforcements who had been on the Argentine submarine. They will all be returned to Argentina. This action in *no* way alters the Government's determination to do *everything possible* to achieve a negotiated settlement to the present crisis. We seek the implementation of the Security Council resolution, and we seek it by *peaceful means.*

Loud chorus of hear-hears! as she sits, and waving of order papers. MICHAEL FOOT *rises.*

SPEAKER: Mr Michael Foot.

FOOT: While joining the Prime Minister's heartfelt relief that the operation was carried out without loss of life, the most important questions remain: *How* are we to pursue the search for a diplomatic settlement, to which the Right Honourable lady has just referred? Do the Argentines yet appreciate that, if they refuse to negotiate, we *will* invade?

A united roar of agreement from both sides of the house.

151. ARGENTINE NEWS-REELS

The Plaza Mayo, outside the Casa Rosada. Members of the dense crowd are hysterical, weeping and waving their fists and screaming at camera over the loss of South Georgia, frenzied with anger and bewilderment.

152. INT. THE OVAL ROOM,THE WHITE HOUSE, WASHINGTON

REAGAN *and* HAIG *are at a little podium for a press conference (as seen on television) – addressing us directly.*

HAIG (*reading out statement*): Gentlemen, the crisis in the South Atlantic is about to enter a new and dangerous phase. In the light of Argentina's failure to accept a compromise, the United States is ending its attempts at mediation. The President has ordered the immediate imposition of a wide range of economic sanctions against Argentina. Moreover, the United States will as of now respond positively to any request by British forces for military assistance.

REAGAN: Gentlemen, we must remember that the aggression was on the part of Argentina in this little dispute over, er . . . that little bunch of ice-cold islands down there. (*crisply*) That's got to be stopped.

153. INT. THE CABINET ROOM

The War Cabinet in session.

PM (*very bullish*): You fly straight over there, Francis, and tell Haig exactly what we need!

PYM: It could be done by tele –

PM: Tell him face-to-face!

PYM: Do you think I should leave my desk just as –

PM (*flatly*): Yes. (*to* ARMSTRONG) Yes?

ARMSTRONG: Total Exclusion Zone.

PM: Attorney?

HAVERS: Admiral Woodward's battle group of twelve warships enters the Maritime Exclusion Zone today. It thereupon becomes a *Total* Exclusion Zone – TEZ. Aircraft as well as ships will be attacked, irrespective of nationality, if they attempt to enter it.

PM: CDS, would you reiterate the object of this?

LEWIN: It's a further tightening of the screw, Prime Minister. Aerial and naval action will be launched over the Falklands, to draw the enemy into combat, before our landing force arrives. There will be a further combination of air activity, shelling of shore positions and naval manoeuvres, all looking like the prelude to an imminent invasion, which will draw out their reserves. Only after that will we actually invade. (*Each member has a copy of a map showing the outline of the zone. They pore over these.*) In connection with this, Prime Minister, may I raise a point?

PM: Of course.

LEWIN: In addition to the TEZ, I think it important we should promulgate a broader warning – that enemy ships or airplanes in *any* position will be attacked if they pose a threat to British forces.

WHITELAW (*growl*): More or less the same thing.

LEWIN (*turning to him*): With respect, they are two distinct things. Anything *in*side the TEZ *will* be attacked; anything outside it *may* be attacked, without warning, if it threatens our forces.

NOTT: How would we inform the Argentines?

HAVERS: Through the United Nations – as we inform them about everything.

WHITELAW: If the Argies could sink one of our carriers, they'd go ahead and do it, no matter where it was!

NOTT: So we'd be placing ourselves on the same footing as them?

WHITELAW: Yes, but doing it publicly, and giving notice.

PM: Very well, Attorney, would you go ahead with such a warning?

LEWIN: One further thing, Prime Minister, if I may.

PM: Of course.

LEWIN: The war cabinet will have read the paper on Operation Blackbuck – the single Vulcan bomber flying from Ascension. The RAF now need to finalize its target.

PM: The runway at Port Stanley, or the military airports on the Argentine mainland?

LEWIN: Exactly.

PM: Attorney, have you anything to say on this?

HAVERS: In my view, either would come within Article 51 of the United Nations Charter, as legitimate acts of pre-emptive self-defence. However, if we bomb the mainland, we run the risk of escalating the conflict to a State of War, whether declared or not. In that case, the Hague Convention would debar the USA from being able to assist us.

WHITELAW: And the object of bombing Stanley airfield . . . ?

LEWIN: To lay a string of small bombs precisely across the runway, one of which will crater it. That would prevent their high-speed planes from taking off to attack our approaching Task Force.

NOTT: What about civilian casualties?

LEWIN: This type of bombing is surgically precise. In my view, the risk is negligible.

WHITELAW: That decides it for me.

PM: Port Stanley?

General agreement.

LEWIN: Four hours later, a general strike on military targets will be carried out by Harriers from the *Hermes* and *Invincible*.

154. ROYAL AIR FORCE FILM

1. Operation Blackbuck – the single plane landing a single small bomb in the centre of the airstrip, from two miles up. 2. Sequence of the Harriers taking off into battle, from the flight deck of the two carriers.

155. INT. THE SECRETARY GENERAL'S ROOM, UN BUILDING, NEW YORK

PEREZ DE CUELLAR, PARSONS *and* COSTA-MENDEZ.

DE CUELLAR: (*considerably worried*): I would like you immediately to convey my offer to both Governments.

PARSONS (*smoothly*): I'm sure my Government will welcome it.

DE CUELLAR: Speed is most important.

COSTA-MENDEZ (*shaking head*): I am not sure how my Government will view a further attempt to mediate.

PARSONS: Not even by the United Nations?!

COSTA-MENDEZ (*sanctimoniously*): After the brutal and unprovoked attack by the RAF –

PARSONS: You invaded! Not us!

COSTA-MENDEZ (*shaking his head, sadly*): Aggression should not be allowed to succeed!

156. INT. THE SECRETARY OF STATE'S OFFICE, STATE DEPARTMENT

HAIG *sits at his desk, considerably agitated.* PYM *is on his feet, angry.*

HAIG: I query the integrity of such a strike! It's grown into a major battle.

PYM: They invaded! Not us!

HAIG: The Argentines have sent in over forty planes to attack your Sea Harriers and ships, are you aware of that? Engaging your Fleet!

PYM *points to a typed sheet on Haig's desk.*

PYM: Will you provide us with the assistance on that list?

HAIG: Of course we will, of course. Meantime . . . (*he gets up*) I could get onto the Government of Peru. *They* could take over Haig Two – maybe they'd listen to another Latin-American country.

PYM: Al, both sides have rejected Haig Two!

HAIG: Well we've got to keep talking! Or the South Atlantic will become a blood-bath!

157. NEWSFILM

The intense air battle, as the greater part of the Argentine air force is hurled in to attack our battle group. The bombardment by five warships commences with a roar.

158. INT. OCR, FLEET HEADQUARTERS, NORTHWOOD

Close shot of the operational map of the South Atlantic. WRENS *move the position of the battle group's ships as they deploy one hundred miles north-west of the Falklands. They also track and plot the suspected positions of the Argentine fleet. Widen to show the whole OCR in operation. The atmosphere is tense, close to the end of the big air battle still being fought. In the foreground, a signal comes up on one of the VDUs. Zoom in on it. 'CONQUERОR TO CINC FLEET. [1] VIS CONTACT ONE ARG. CRUISER AND TWO ESCORTS. [2] IDENTIFIED BELGRANO POS 551703 S 611617 WMLA 120 SP 12. [3] APN CRUISER WD APPEAR TO BE IN DEFENCE WATCHES. FLASH 011340 SITREP FFS.' Tighten on the word 'Belgrano'. Cut to* FIELDHOUSE *as he receives and reads this signal print-out. He immediately turns to the big operational map, on which* A WREN *is just moving markers which reflect the new information. Markers labelled 'Conqueror' 'Belgrano' and two labelled 'Tanker' are moved into position.* FIELDHOUSE *stares at the map, taking in the grouping of the British battle group between what is starting to look like the two halves of the Argentine fleet, north and south.*

159. INT. SECRETARY OF STATE'S OFFICE, STATE DEPARTMENT

HAIG *on the telephone,* ENDERS *with earpiece.*

HAIG (*muttering*): Come on, come on.

ENDERS: Telephones in Peru are still made of jungle creeper.

Interjections in Spanish, and then an authoritative voice is heard.

BELAUNDE (*distort*): General Haig?

HAIG: Good evening, Mr President, I very much appreciate the chance to talk to you, sir.

160. INT. BELAUNDE'S STUDY, LIMA

Close shot of BELAUNDE *head and shoulders only.*

BELAUNDE: What can I do for you?

HAIG (*distort*): I have a seven-point conceptualization I would like to put to you, sir, to end hostilities in the South Atlantic.

BELAUNDE: You put to *me*?

161. INT. OCR, FLEET HEADQUARTERS, NORTHWOOD

Close shot of FIELDHOUSE, *trying to snatch forty winks in a chair. A* SENIOR OFFICER *comes up, signal print-out in hand.*

SENIOR OFFICER: Sir. (FIELDHOUSE *grunts, wakes, takes the signal.*) Can I get you some coffee, sir?

FIELDHOUSE: Yes please.

He rubs his eyes and reads the signal. Concerned, he rises to the edge of the 'balcony' and examines the big operational map facing him. A WREN *is just moving markers in the northern sector – showing that the main group of Argentine warships has moved past the two British nuclear-powered submarines* Spartan *and* Splendid *which patrol the north edge of the TEZ. Close shot of* FIELDHOUSE, *pondering this.*

162. INT. MINISTERIAL CAR

LEWIN *and* FIELDHOUSE *in the back, small operational chart on their knees.*

FIELDHOUSE: The *Veinticinco de Mayo* and her escorts slipped down to here (*points*) during the night. Their main battle force.

LEWIN: But how did they get past our nuclear subs?

He indicates the arc of their patrol line.

FIELDHOUSE: I don't know. Visibility is very bad, but a Sea Harrier picked up emissions of the radar on their Type 42s and found them. The satellite pictures confirm it.

LEWIN: Have you spoken to Woodward?

FIELDHOUSE: Yes. He's convinced it's a pincer movement. *(He indicates what he means with finger and thumb on the chart.)* He wants *Belgrano* sunk. (LEWIN *studies the chart, concerned.)*

163. INT. THE PRIME MINISTER'S STUDY, CHEQUERS

The PM *has the chart.* LEWIN *and* FIELDHOUSE *are with her.*

PM: Pincer movement?

FIELDHOUSE (*indicating*): The *Belgrano*, and her escorts, carrying Exocets, could suddenly turn and steam hard north. The *Veinticinco de Mayo* could simultaneously steam south and launch her Skyhawk attack aircraft. Both our carriers would be caught in the middle.

PM: What is the answer?

LEWIN: Pick off one arm of the pincer.

PM: Yes?

LEWIN: *Conqueror* should sink *Belgrano.*

The PM *is deeply concerned; this would be a major escalation of the war.*

PM: Can we leave such a decision until a pincer movement has actually started?

LEWIN: Here (*he indicates*) is the Birdwood Bank, of shallow water. If *Belgrano* turns north, she'll be over that very quickly; it's deep enough for her, but too shallow for a submarine to follow. The chance would have gone.

PM: Hm. We've got a War Cabinet at three.

LEWIN: We've got to order this now, Prime Minister.

PM: Well, everyone's arriving for the meeting. Round them up.

164. INT. THE GREAT PARLOUR (MAIN ROOM), CHEQUERS

Senior civil servants, service chiefs and Cabinet ministers are standing around with pre-lunch drinks in hand, chattering noisily. LEWIN *and* FIELDHOUSE *enter and hurriedly detach the members of the War Cabinet, directing them to the little alcove at the far end of the room.*

165. INT. THE GREAT PARLOUR (ALCOVE), CHEQUERS

LEWIN, NOTT ,WHITELAW, HAVERS, ARMSTRONG *and the* PRIME MINISTER *(not Pym or Fieldhouse.) They are all standing up in a little ring in this small room, some still with drinks in hand. There is a general air of shock at what is being proposed.*

WHITELAW: What about loss of life?!

LEWIN (*quietly*): There are bound to be casualties, yes. She might only be disabled; but if she sank, the two escorts could rescue the ship's company.

WHITELAW (*mutters*): Those who survived.

PM (*to* LEWIN): Are we *absolutely* certain she is armed with Exocet?

LEWIN: Not one hundred per cent. But there have been intelligence reports that she is.

NOTT: We have to assume they are correct.

LEWIN: Her escorts certainly are.

PM: How can we be certain that they intend to attack in the way you anticipate?

LEWIN: Our appreciation is that they intend an all-out attack on the Task Force now that it has arrived – air, surface ships and submarines. Their shorebased aircraft bombed our ships yesterday. *Glamorgan* was near-missed. They claimed to have hit *Hermes*, but didn't. We hunted a submarine that was certainly in a position to attack. We must expect another attack, probably coordinated, today.

WHITELAW: But this ship is *out*side the TEZ!

HAVERS: Oh, that's clearly covered by our warning of 23 April – anything outside it *may* be attacked, without warning, if it constitutes a threat.

NOTT: What about the direction the *Belgrano* is steaming?

LEWIN: That means nothing – she can change course in thirty seconds. The one thing she *won't* do is betray the course she's going to take when the pincer is sprung, until the last moment.

HAVERS: What's her complement?

LEWIN: About a thousand men.

PM: The threat is clear, I think we should consider the political implications.

HAVERS: There's bound to be tremendous world reaction. It would be a major escalation of the fighting.

PM: But they've been trying to sink our ships, kill our boys! *They* invaded, not us! – and they attacked us yesterday.

NOTT: I don't think we've any alternative.

PM: Willy?

WHITELAW: I agree.

PM: Attorney?

HAVERS (*still troubled*): I don't have enough information to offer a legal opinion.

PM: You said it would be clearly within our Warning of 23 April.

HAVERS: Oh, it's certainly that. (*to* LEWIN) Suppose the

Conqueror kept shadowing her, if necessary going *round* the Birdwood Bank?

LEWIN: She would almost certainly lose her.

HAVERS: Then I agree.

PM (*to* LEWIN): How quickly would this happen?

LEWIN: The signal can go out now. Then it's up to the *Conqueror.*

166. INT. BELAUNDE'S STUDY, LIMA

Close shot of Belaunde – head and shoulders only.

BELAUNDE (*on telephone*): General? I am very glad to have the chance to talk to you, General Galtieri. I wish to put certain proposals to you that I believe could be the basis of a peaceful settlement in the South Atlantic . . .

167. INT. THE PRESIDENT'S STUDY, CASA ROSADA

GALTIERI, ANAYA, DOZO, COSTA-MENDEZ *and* ROS *around the conference table. They each have typed copies of the seven-point plan, and a good deal of Glenfiddich.*

DOZO: I do not see how this could be possible!

ROS: It is Haig all over again! Haig Two!

GALTIERI: Exactly! That is what I told him.

ROS: Certain details have been altered . . . item six, for example: the contact group is now Brazil, Peru, West Germany and the USA, that is a little different.

ANAYA (*shrugging*): They are differences that make no matter.

COSTA-MENDEZ: But now we are at war, we stand in a different position!

GALTIERI: No. It is the same. No difference. (*They all reread *the proposals, gloomily. As they do so,* A SENIOR OFFICER *enters quietly with a signal print-out for* ANAYA. GALTIERI *continues grandly.*) To accept this would be to sacrifice our honour!

ANAYA *has gone white.*

ANAYA (*abruptly*): The British have hit the *Belgrano.*

DOZO: What?

ANAYA: Two torpedoes. She's sinking.

He runs out of the room. GALTIERI *snatches up the signal, and reads for himself, incredulously. No one speaks.*

168. INT. HOUSE OF COMMONS

NOTT *at the despatch box. The* PRIME MINISTER *sits grimly beside him, on the front bench.*

NOTT: . . . it is feared the loss of life may have been heavy. Our submarine did not attack the two escorting destroyers, in the belief that they would assist survivors. Regrettably, the escorts rapidly removed themselves from the scene. The loss of life must be a matter of deep concern to the House, but our first duty must be the protection of our ships and men! The way to stop the fighting is for the Argentines to withdraw their garrison, in compliance with United Nation Resolution 502.

He sits. FOOT *rises.*

SPEAKER: Mr Foot.

FOOT: Can the Right Honourable lady tell us what political control there was over this major development? Is there not a grave danger that such an event as the sinking of a ship might recur?

The PM *rises slowly to the despatch box. She is very subdued.*

PM: I assure the Right Honourable gentleman that the Task Force is under full political control. (*Pause. Then she adds, quietly, straight from the heart.*) The worry I live with hourly is that attacking Argentine forces may get through to ours, and sink some of *our* ships.

169. INT. THE SECRETARY OF STATE'S ROOM, STATE DEPARTMENT

HAIG, HENDERSON *and* WALTERS.

WALTERS: Naturally, we wonder what effect this may have on the Peruvian peace plan.

HENDERSON: 'Haig in a poncho.'

HAIG: Pardon me?

HENDERSON: That's what the Argies are calling it.

HAIG: I like it! 'Haig in a poncho'!

He writes it down, chuckling to himself.

HENDERSON: Buenos Aires is continuing to negotiate. The *Belgrano* has made no difference to that.

HAIG: That's for sure?

HENDERSON (*nodding*): They've just confirmed next week's schedule of meetings with Perez de Cuellar.

HAIG *brightens at this. He can't resist it.*

HAIG: Then maybe I should have one last try . . .

WALTERS: Now, Mr Secretary . . .

HAIG: Well maybe not me. Maybe *you* should go, Dick, and try talking to that bunch of drunken screwballs down there. We don't want them talking to the Soviets.

WALTERS (*grimacing*): If you say so, sir.

HAIG: Secretly, of course.

170. INT. THE CABINET ROOM

The War Cabinet in session. LEWIN *is at the easel map stand.*

LEWIN: There's no doubt of the effect on the Argentine Navy. Every one of their ships has scuttled back here . . . (*he indicates the coastal strip along the mainland*) . . . where the water is too shallow for our subs to operate. It's effectively neutralized their entire Fleet.

WHITELAW (*for the PM's benefit*): Thus probably *saving* lives. (*Silence.* THE PM *makes no response.*) Margaret.

PM (*coming to*): Yes sorry. Attorney?

HAVERS: The new TEZ – leaving them a twelve-mile strip down the coast – will effectively pin them in.

Silence. Members of the War Cabinet look across at the PM. *She is deeply preoccupied.*

171. INT. THE PRIME MINISTER'S ROOM, HOUSE OF COMMONS

The PM *working alone, at her place on the half-size Cabinet table, facing the big window. She is unable to concentrate, as if waiting for something. The room is completely silent and still. A buzz on the intercom.*

PM: Yes?

SECRETARY (*distort*): May the Minister of Defence see you urgently, Prime Minister?

PM: Yes.

JOHN NOTT *enters quietly, signal in hand. The* PM *does not turn to greet him. He walks over to stand beside her at the table.*

NOTT (*quietly*): The *Sheffield*'s been hit. We think by an Exocet. There may be a lot of casualties.

The PM *says nothing. Her hands clench and unclench, she arches her head back and the tears silently flood down her face.*

172. INT. HOUSE OF COMMONS

Eleven o'clock at night. The sparsely-filled house is stunned. JOHN NOTT *is at the despatch box. Beside him sits the* PM, *dressed in black from head to foot, the picture of grief.*

NOTT: . . . The ship caught fire, which soon spread out of control. The order was given to abandon ship. Communications within the operational area are difficult at present. Next of kin will, of course, be informed, as soon as we have information.

He sits. FOOT *rises.*

SPEAKER: Mr Foot.

FOOT (*gravely*): I do not seek, in this moment of tragedy, to make any *political* comment; but I hope the Government will make a full statement tomorrow, so that we can debate the matter.

He sits. This marker that he intends to try and score some party-political points out of this event, coming at such a moment, shocks the Tory benches. A back-bencher stands.

SPEAKER: Mr Wells.

JOHN WELLS (*shaking with anger, shouting*): One cannot help feeling that the Leader of the Opposition is a prize hypocrite on –

Instantly the house erupts over the rest of the sentence, its shock exploding into anger both for and against the speaker. Several members jump to their feet, shouting simultaneously, waving their order papers. Slow zoom in on the PRIME MINISTER, *deaf to this hubbub, sitting motionless.*

173. INT. THE PRESIDENT'S STUDY, CASA ROSADA

WALTERS *is with the junta. There is an elegiac mood, of defeated men.*

WALTERS (*gently*): Is it not possible to abandon the fighting and break through now, with honour?

GALTIERI: Hundreds have been killed. What can I tell my people they have gained?

WALTERS: I don't know who will be the winner in the Malvinas, but Russia will be the only winner of this war.

Silence as the junta digest this.

DOZO: They are offering military help at a very low price – but we know what the real price would be.

ANAYA: I will never, repeat, never, turn to the Soviet Union. (*He turns his gaze fully on* WALTERS, *and whispers*) Three hundred and sixty-eight of my sailors died in the *Belgrano*. They are my sons. I will not betray them.

WALTERS *nods, slowly, gravely.*

174. INT. THE GREAT PARLOUR, CHEQUERS

HAVERS *knocks and enters, with* HENDERSON *and* PARSONS. *He is surprised not to find the PM there.* ARMSTRONG *is putting out some papers for her attention, in her usual neat and ordered spot.*

ARMSTRONG: She's gone out for a walk.

HAVERS: A walk?!

ARMSTRONG *indicates the window.* HAVERS *crosses to it, and looks out.*

175. EXT. MEADOWS AND PARKLAND

A solitary figure can be seen, walking in the distance, slightly hunched, occasionally swinging an arm askant, like a grieving child.

176. INT. THE GREAT PARLOUR, CHEQUERS

The War Cabinet, sitting with PARSONS *and* HENDERSON. *They all have copies of Perez de Cuellar's proposals. The* PM *is far, far tougher and more resolute. The experiences of the last few days and this, the final crossroads, have roused a fiery impatience in her.*

PM: It is the last chance. If we fail to get a deal on the UN proposals, a great many more people are going to be killed. General comments. Home Secretary?

WHITELAW: It goes far further than we've gone before. Abandoning sovereignty, agreeing to a United Nations Governor . . .

PM (*blistering*): I am aware of what it says, what is your position?

WHITELAW: I suppose it's acceptable. As a last-ditch try.

PARSONS: It leaves many matters very vague, Prime Minister.

PM: Surely that is Perez de Cuellar's intention!

PARSONS: Everything must be clear, no one must be –

PM: For Heaven's sake, we're trying to –

PARSONS (*standing his ground*): If you would allow me to finish, Prime Minister, I think you might agree with me. It's up to you and the War Cabinet to decide how far you are prepared to go, but it's up to *me* to tell you what this actually says or fails to say.

PM: If you will –

PARSONS (*firmly*): Shall we go through it point by point?

177. ON BOARD PLANE

PARSONS *and* HENDERSON *sit side by side (returning to Washington). They each have copies of the final retyped draft.*

HENDERSON (*turning to him*): You were very brave.

PARSONS: She's quite the most wonderful and quite the most impossible human being I've ever met. While she was talking, I kept on remembering 'Little man, little man, *must* is not a word to use to Princes'.

HENDERSON: You know, she's written scores of letters in her own hand, to the families of every single serviceman killed. She'll go on doing that as long as the fighting lasts.

PARSONS (*quietly*): That may be a lot of letters.

HENDERSON *grunts. They both turn back to the draft, in silence.*

178. INT. THE SECURITY COUNCIL CHAMBER, UN BUILDING, NEW YORK. NIGHT

Most of the lights are out. Only two people are present – ROS, *who sits at his delegation desk, with a copy of the draft proposals; and* JEAN KIRKPATRICK, *who is walking about, shouting.*

KIRKPATRICK: It would be self-defeating madness to reject it! It's all there!

ROS: I don't know . . .

KIRKPATRICK (*shouting*): Enrique, it really constitutes what Argentina wants! Accept it, and you'd have won!

ROS: Not as simple as that . . .

179. INTERCUTTING THE SECRETARY OF STATE'S ROOM, STATE DEPARTMENT/THE FOREIGN SECRETARY'S ROOM, FOREIGN OFFICE

PYM *and* HAIG *are on the telephone to each other. It is late at night.*

HAIG: If they reject it, I could come up with another proposal . . .

PYM: Al, we've been negotiating for six and a half weeks. The Argentines can't deliver!

HAIG (*desperately*): But I can't seriously believe you'd invade! In three days?

180. INT. THE CABINET ROOM

Close shot of a detailed tactical plan of the Falkland Islands, on which is marked the entire scheme for 'Operation Corporate'. LEWIN *and* FIELDHOUSE, *in full uniform, are with the* PM *and* JOHN NOTT.

LEWIN: We think it will take about an hour to explain the plan to the full Cabinet – from the landing here at San Carlos, to the capture of Port Stanley.

PM: How much notice would you require?

LEWIN: For the landing?

PM: No no, explaining this.

LEWIN: Only how long it would take to get here. It's all ready.

NOTT: We haven't yet heard from the UN, you see.

LEWIN: Could there be a last-minute agreement?

The PM *doesn't reply.*

PM: Where is the Task Force now?

FIELDHOUSE (*pointing*): Here. On full battle alert. (*turns to* PM) Waiting for us.

181. INT. THE SECURITY COUNCIL CHAMBER, UN BUILDING

PARSONS, *alone at his desk in the otherwise empty chamber. He is writing a letter. The telephone beneath his desk buzzes. He picks it up.*

PARSONS: Parsons.

DE CUELLAR (*distort*): I have the Argentine reply. Perhaps you would care to wait till the morning . . . ?

PARSONS: I'll come now.

182. INT. THE SECRETARY-GENERAL'S CONFERENCE ROOM, UN BUILDING

PARSONS *enters.* PEREZ DE CUELLAR *is mixing two dry martinis.*

DE CUELLAR: It's on the table.

PARSONS: Thank you.

DE CUELLAR: Dry martini?

PARSONS *plucks up the single typed sheet on the table and reads. It is clear that it constitutes a complete rejection by Argentina.*

PARSONS (*mutter*): Even sovereignty.

DE CUELLAR *comes over with the drinks.*

DE CUELLAR: I hope you have a clear conscience.

PARSONS (*in rage and exasperation*): Even sovereignty!

183. INT. THE PRIME MINISTER'S STUDY, 10 DOWNING STREET. NIGHT.

The PM *works by herself in a pool of desk light. She is writing letters in her own hand. Buzz on the intercom.*

PM: Yes?

SECRETARY: Can the Foreign Secretary see you?

PM: Oh. Yes.

PYM *enters. The* PM *is not best pleased to see him.*

PYM: What time do the first troops go in?

PM: 3.40 in the morning. (PYM *looks at his watch.*) I'm not enjoying it either.

PYM: We won't get any real news for some hours.

PM: I know.

PYM: And it's not a question of 'enjoying it'. It's more . . . (*he gestures*) . . . it can't be right.

PM (*gritting her teeth*): What can't be right?

PYM: Trying to settle anything by warfare. It's appalling.

PM: *They* invaded.

PYM: Of course, but –

PM: What should we do, lie down and let them trample all over those people?

PYM: What people?

PM: The Falkland Islanders! The people they invaded, the people who desperately want to stay British!

PYM: I don't know anything about international law, but it seems to me it must be the most criminal act, in 1982, to *decide* to go to war, as we have, calmly decide to kill people –

The PM *finally explodes in anger.*

PM: Only one thing makes war justified, and lawful, only one thing! – when it's a struggle for law against force – for the life of those people, their laws, their language and way of life, everything that makes them what they are, against a brutal effort to impose on them a life and language and laws that are not theirs and they do not want! – when everything else has been tried, and failed! – *not* because of us! If we are wrong to fight now, then we were wrong to fight Hitler, we were wrong to fight the Kaiser, we were wrong to fight Napoleon, we were wrong to fight Philip of Spain – wrong to do anything but throw in the towel and crumple before the first brute force to come along, and abandon all the fine and good and splendid things Britain has given the world down the centuries, for a bleak, totalitarian desert!

PYM *has listened to this, hunched and inscrutable, waiting for her to finish. Her speech has made not the slightest impression on him.*

PYM (*mutter*): Well, I just hope you're right, that's all.

With a shout of rage, the PM *flings her arms wide in exasperation!*

184. SPECTACULAR MONTAGE

The War itself. A montage of three elements: 1. The main events in the fighting (news-film: San Carlos, Goose Green, Bluff Cove, Port Stanley); 2. Ian MacDonald intoning and announcing the main events; 3. The Pope's visits at the height of the war, to Great Britain and to Argentina (news-film).

185. INT. THE PRIME MINISTER'S ROOM, HOUSE OF COMMONS

ARMSTRONG, WHITELAW, *the* PM *and* LEWIN, *round the half-size Cabinet Table.* ARMSTRONG *is working with the* PM, *drafting her statement to the House.* LEWIN *is on the telephone, holding on. Confused, long-distance noises are coming over the line – distant shouts, some gunshots, conversation just too far off to hear. It is a direct line to Port Stanley. Suddenly,* FIELDHOUSE *is heard, close.*

FIELDHOUSE (*distort*): They've signed.

LEWIN (*to the PM*): They've signed.

The PM looks up, grinning like a schoolgirl.

186. INT. HOUSE OF COMMONS

The House is in session. The PM *brings* LEWIN *in by the private entrance behind the Speaker's chair – the shortest way from her room. It is much darker here. She puts him in a particular spot, from which he can see the government front bench.*

PM: You watch from here.

She moves into the House itself. As soon as she appears, there is loud cheering and waving of order papers. She takes her seat with a smile. THE MEMBER SPEAKING *stops and sits.*

SPEAKER: The Prime Minister.

The PM *rises to the despatch box.*

PM: Mr Speaker, I will with permission make a short statement about the Falkland Islands. After successful attacks last night, General Moore decided to press forward. The Argentines retreated. Our forces reached the outskirts of Port Stanley. Large numbers of Argentine soldiers threw down their weapons. They are reported to be flying white flags over Port Stanley –

That is as far as she can get. The House erupts in an explosion of cheering, long and loud. Members are on their feet, waving order papers. It finally subsides. FOOT *rises.*

SPEAKER: Mr Foot.

FOOT: May I thank the Right Honourable lady for coming to the House to give us the news, particularly as it will mean an end to the bloodshed. There will be great congratulations from the House tomorrow to the British forces who have conducted themselves so magnificently, and, if I may say so, to the Right Honourable lady herself.

Loud hear, hears! He sits.

SPEAKER: Mr Wedgwood Benn.

BENN (*rising*): Will the Prime Minister publish a full analysis of the costs in life, equipment and money of this tragic and unnecessary war, which the world knows very well will not provide an answer to the problems of the Falkland Islands?

PM: The Right Honourable gentleman calls it an unnecessary war. Tragic it may have been, but may I point out to him – (*she suddenly flings out her arm and points at him, shouting;*

it is her true moment of celebration and triumph) – he would not enjoy the freedom of speech that he puts to such excellent use, unless people had been prepared to fight for it!

The House roars like the sea. Freeze frame on her triumphal gesture.

BLACKOUT

A NOTE ON SOURCES

My sources were threefold: a) printed sources, listed below; b) interviews with some of the main participants in the crisis; c) my own dramatic craft and imagination.

I was allowed to visit Chequers, 10 Downing Street, the Ministry of Defence, the Prime Minister's room in the House of Commons, Fleet Headquarters at Northwood, the Foreign Secretary's room in the Foreign Office, and other locations.

Every fact in the play is based on authentic printed sources, of which the following were most significant.

Official Sources

The Franks Report. Franks, Baron Oliver Shewell Franks, *Falkland Islands Review: Report of a Committee of Privy Counsellors*, (Cmnd; 8787), HMSO, 1983

Foreign Affairs Committee, 1984–5 session, (House of Commons) third report, 'Events surrounding the week-end of 1–2 May 1982' (HC II)

Hansard, House of Commons, December 1980–June 1982; House of Lords, April–June 1982

Organization of American States (OAS), minutes of proceedings, April–June 1982

United Nations Security Council, minutes of meetings 2345 (1 April 1982)–2373 (4 June 1982)

Journals and newspapers

The Economist, 2–8 June 1979, pp. 29–40

The Economist, 12 November 1983, pp. 49–60

The Falklands War, part 1–14, Marshall Cavendish, 1983

New Statesman, 25 January 1985, pp. 8–10
Newsweek, 7 June 1982, pp. 29–31
Observer, passim, 1982–5
Sunday Times, passim, 1982–5
The Times, complete coverage, April–June 1982

Biographies

Cosgrave, Patrick, *Carrington: A Life and a Policy*, Dent, 1985
Cosgrave, Patrick, *Margaret Thatcher*, Hutchinson, 1978
Haig, Alexander, *Caveat: Realism, Reagan and Foreign Policy*, Weidenfeld & Nicolson, 1984
Henderson, Sir Nicholas, *The Private Office*, Weidenfeld & Nicolson, 1984
Murray, Patricia, *Margaret Thatcher*, W. H. Allen, 1980
Thomas, George, *Mr Speaker: The Memoirs of the Viscount Tonypandy*, Century, 1985
The Times, *Sunday Times* and *Observer*, miscellaneous press profiles

Places and institutions

Fry, P. Somerset, *Chequers: the Country Home of Britain's Prime Ministers*, HMSO, 1977
Jones, Christopher, *Number Ten Downing Street: the Story of a House*, BBC Publications, 1985
Sampson, Anthony, *The New Anatomy of Britain*, Hodder & Stoughton, 1982
The Times Guide to the House of Commons, June 1983, Times, 1984
Walker, Patrick Gordon, *The Cabinet*, Cape, 1970
Williams, Marcia, *Inside Number 10*, Weidenfeld & Nicolson, 1972

The war itself

Barnett, Anthony, *Iron Britannia*, Allison & Busby, 1982
Bishop, Patrick and Witherow, John, *The Winter War: the Falklands*, Quartet, 1982
Critchley, M., *Falklands Task Force Portfolio*, Maritime Books, 1982
Dalyell, Tam, *One Man's Falklands*, Cecil Woolf, 1982
Dalyell, Tam, *Thatcher's Torpedo*, Cecil Woolf, 1983
Fox, Robert, *Eyewitness Falklands*, Methuen, 1982
Gavshon, Arthur and Rice, Desmond, *The Sinking of the Belgrano*, Secker & Warburg, 1984
Harris, Robert, *Gotcha! The Media, the Government and the Falklands Crisis*, Faber & Faber, 1983
Hastings, Max and Jenkins, Simon, *The Battle for the Falklands*, Michael Joseph, 1983
Laffin, John, *Fight for the Falklands*, Chivers, 1982
McGowan, Robert and Hands, Jeremy, *Don't Cry for Me, Sergeant-Major*, Futura, 1983
Middlebrook, Martin, *Operation Corporate: the Falklands War, 1982*, Viking, 1985
Sunday Times Insight team, the, *The Falklands War*, Deutsch, 1982
Tinker, David, *A Message from the Falklands: the Life and Gallant Death of*, compiled by Hugh Tinker, Penguin, 1983

Miscellaneous

Buenos Aires y sus Esculturas
Cockerell, Michael, Hennessy, Peter and Walker, David, *Sources Close to the Prime Minister*, Macmillan, 1984
Ferguson, J. Halcro, *The River Plate Republics*
Giacobbe, Juan Francisco, *Viejo Buenos Aires*
Mujica, Manuel Lainez, *Letra e Imagen de Buenos Aires*, Ediciones Libreria La Ciudad, 1977
Ocampo, Silvina, *Arboles de Buenos Aires*, Ediciones Libreria La Ciudad, 1979

Speed, Keith, *Sea Change: the Battle for the Falklands and the Future of Britain's Navy*, Ashgrove, 1982
Street Map of Buenos Aires